Alexander W Winter

Packers' and Refiners' Encyclopedia

For the Practical Use of Pork Packers, Lard Refiners, Butchers and Beef Slaughterers

and pork and cattle raisers throughout the world

Alexander W Winter

Packers' and Refiners' Encyclopedia
For the Practical Use of Pork Packers, Lard Refiners, Butchers and Beef Slaughterers and pork and cattle raisers throughout the world

ISBN/EAN: 9783337144920

Printed in Europe, USA, Canada, Australia, Japan

Cover: Foto ©Andreas Hilbeck / pixelio.de

More available books at **www.hansebooks.com**

PACKERS' *AND* REFINERS'

ENCYCLOPEDIA

For the Practical use of Pork Packers, Lard Refiners, Butchers and
Beef Slaughterers, and Pork and Cattle Raisers
throughout the World

Containing the Latest Processes and Formulas for making all
grades of Lards and for Bleaching, Deodorizing and
Clarifying Lards, Tallow, Greases and Oils; also
for manufacturing Fertilizers and caring
for the Bones, Blood and Offal, as well
as for the manufacture of Oleomargarine, Butterine, etc.

BY

ALEX. W. WINTER

Fully Illustrated

CHICAGO
LAIRD & LEE, PUBLISHERS
1893

PACKERS' AND REFINERS' ENCYCLOPEDIA

Outline of Contents.

Lard Department of the Packing House.

Processes for manufacturing lards:

    Pure kettle lard.

    Prime steam.

    Choice family.

    Cottoline.

    Lard compound.

    Silver leaf.

    Imitation steam lard.

    Cuba lard.

    Watered lard.

Processes for refining lard.

Processes for bleaching lard, oils, tallow and greases.

Processes for deodorizing the same.

Processes for clarifying the same.

Suggestions as to machinery used in these processes.

How to pack lard.

    Size of packages used.

How to put crimp lard to imitate pure kettle leaf.

At what temperature lard should be pumped through the filter.

How to properly fit up the filter so it can be readily cleaned without the loss of a particle of lard.

At what temperature to run lard over the roller.

At what temperature water should go into the roller.

At what temperature to draw lard from the agitator.

At what temperature to cool lard so as to prevent cracking.

Special table for figuring hardness for different climates, so that in shipping to warm or cold countries the lard will be of proper texture.

Best formulas for making lards that will not crumble.

European formulas.

Best modes of rendering tallow with water and steam.

How to harden tallow.

How to bleach tallow by exposure and by chemicals.

Machinery required for making oleomargarine.

Selection and preparation of fats for oleomargarine.

How to manufacture oleomargarine, oleo oil, oleo butter and butterine

Chemical comparison between oleo butter and natural butter.

How to prepare the leaf for making neutral.

How to make wet and dry neutral.

Laws of the different states governing the manufacture and sale of oleomargarine.

Latest and most improved modes of caring for bones, blood and offal.

Very latest machinery for same.

How glycerine is obtained and manufactured into a chemically pure article

How to make fatty acid tests.

Purification and bleaching of fatty acids.

Best grades of cotton-seed oil.

Specific gravity and congealing point of refined cotton-seed oil.

Best brand of Fuller's earth to use and where it comes from.

Chemical analysis and properties of the best Fuller's earth.

Refrigerating machines for small packing houses.

How to adulterate oils.

How to arrange catch-basins so as to avoid loss of grease in washing floors.

Free acid tests.

Solution and glasses required for making free acid tests.

Delicate method of obtaining per cent stearic acid, oleic acid, in tallow, greases, etc.

Making sweet pickle for curing meats.

Dry salting meats.

Packers' rendering tanks.

Butchers' tanking outfit.

How to cool a meat market with brine circulating system.

Many other and valuable receipts, processes and practical suggestions most useful to the trade.

The entire contents of the work in detail will be alphabetically indexed, with reference to pages, at the end of the book, making the whole a work of ready reference regarding every important topic connected with the trade.

PREFACE.

DURING the twenty and more years of my experience as a Packing House and Lard Refinery Expert and Specialist, I have received thousands of letters from different parts of the United States and the world, inquiring for information in regard to the various processes and formulas now in use among the most successful Packers and Refiners in this country. My object in preparing the PACKERS' AND REFINERS' ENCYCLOPÆDIA is to furnish, at a nominal cost to the purchaser, a most needed and valuable compendium for all interested in this line of business. Pork Packing and Lard Refining have grown to enormous proportions, and the successful processes have been known to but few in the business, creating almost a monopoly. In my occupation as an expert, I have been paid by large packers as much as $3,500 for a single formula, with no conditions binding me not to convey the same information to others. For some processes I have also received $1,500 each on similar arrangements. Hundreds of thousands of dollars have been expended by Pork Packers and Lard Refiners in experiments and they have received most profitable returns for their investments in this way.

This book gives, in a clear and concise manner, the net results of this vast expenditure and places all known processes in the reach of every one.

Only the most perfect processes and the best formulas in existence are presented in this Encyclopædia, so that no one concerned may be hereafter uncertain as to the results of his own efforts in this line.

As will be seen at first glance, theoretical discussions and extended chemical analyses are omitted as far as possible and only workable methods given. Statements of processes and formulas and full explanations of every necessary feature are put herein in the most lucid form, so that any one who can read may understand. This work is intended for every person connected with the Pork Packing and Lard Refinery business in any capacity whatever, and it will also prove of the greatest assistance to thousands who are but indirectly concerned with the business and yet are in quest of some information which may be of invaluable service to them in their daily occupation.

In conclusion I would say, that during the past years I have been Superintendent and Manager of the Mission Soap and Candle Works, San Francisco, Cal.; Bay Soap and Candle Works, San Francisco; Superintendent and Manager for the Commercial Manufacturing Co., manufacturing Oleomargarine etc., a concern incorporated with a capital of $10,000,000; Superintendent of the Electric Candle Co., of New York; Refiner for the Armour Packing Company, Kansas City. I have also fitted up the refineries of Swift & Company, Chicago; T. E. Wells Company, Chicago; International Packing and Provision Company, Chicago; Minneapolis Provision Company, Minneapolis; Parker, Webb & Co., Detroit, Michigan; Ed. Haakinson & Co., Sioux City, Iowa; Jacob Packing Company, Cincinnati; Masterman & Co., Montreal; Thomas Lowry & Son, Hamilton, Ontario; and others. No literary merit is claimed for this book, but that it will prove the most useful and practical work of its kind to be found in any language is the purpose and expectation of the author.

ALEXANDER W. WINTER.

CHICAGO, March, 1893.

Publishers' Announcement.

WE are much pleased to be able to announce to the public that, by a large outlay of money, we have been able to secure the original and never published manuscript of Mr. Alex. W. Winter's **Packers' and Refiners' Encyclopædia,** a work absolutely unique in its contents and character, and the immense value of which will be apparent, at the very first glance, to any one at all interested in such matters.

The author is a gentleman of world-wide reputation in that particular branch of manufacturing, than which there is none that has grown, in late years, to such enormous proportions.

His experience in the business is so reliable that many a Pork Packer and Lard Refiner owes to him and to the formulas he purchased from him—every one of which is contained in this volume—the origin of a large fortune; and the field is still wide open for others to follow in those footsteps and make these formulas the basis of rapidly accumulated wealth under the circumstances; and, it being well known that none of these precious formulas is to be found in print anywhere else, we think that our issuing Mr. Alex. W. Winter's **Packers' and Refiners' Encyclopædia,** in this finished style and at such a low price, considering the real, high value of it, is sure to secure for it a hearty and widespread welcome.

THE PUBLISHERS.

Blowing Pump for Agitating Lard.

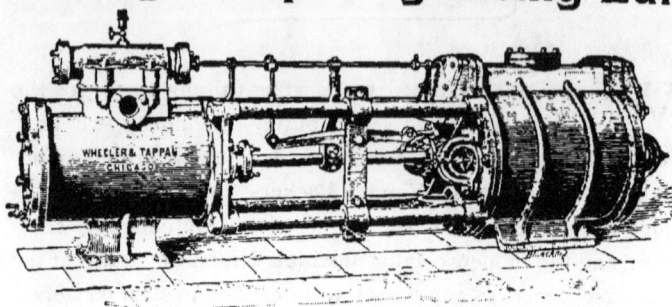

DUPLEX LARD PUMP.

REFINERS' IMPROVED DOUBLE HEAD FILTER PRESS.

50-leaf, size 36x36.   Weight 12 Tons.

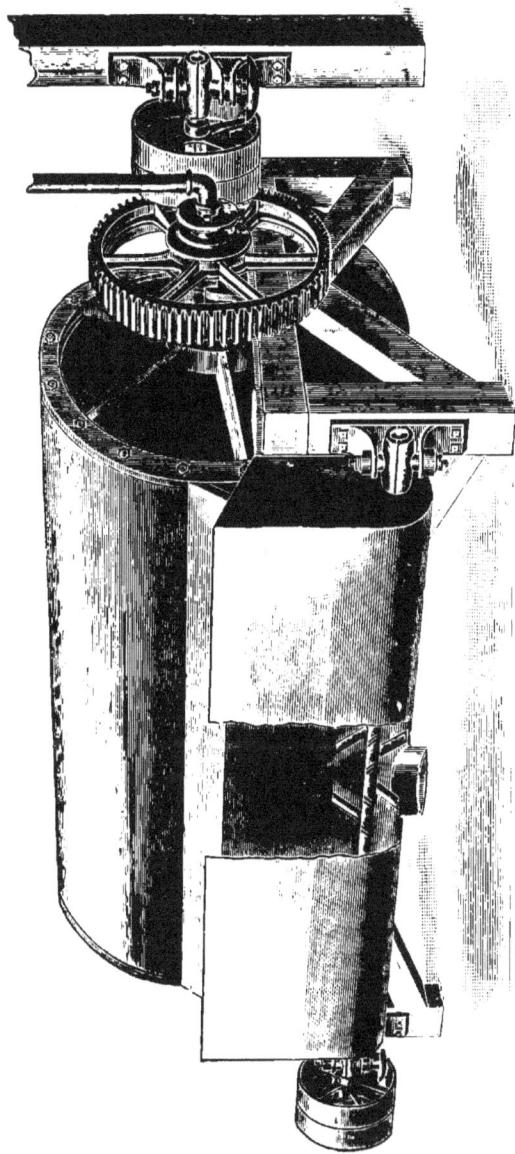

This Cooler consists of a hollow cast iron cylinder turned on the outside perfectly smooth and is 4 feet diameter by 9 feet long. This cylinder is supported by heavy cast iron trunnions on the heads, which run in pillow blocks on the frame work.

The cylinder is made to revolve by means of gears as shown in cut, the pinion shaft of which is fitted with tight and loose pulleys.

The cylinder trunnions are also made hollow for the purpose of receiving the cooling-water, which is pumped in one end at a temperature of 33° F. and overflows through the other, the pipes being arranged so as to keep the cylinder perfectly full and at as even a temperature all through as possible.

A large pan is fitted underneath this revolving cylinder into which the lard is run at a temperature of 100° F. The cold surface of cylinder passing through same cools it instantly to 70° and it also adheres to same, and is carried around until it meets a scraper, which scrapes it off into a galvanized trough which contains a right and left hand conveyor. This conveyor breaks up the lard, and passes it down through a hole in center of trough, from where it can be put at once into packages for shipment.

The machine runs about 16 revolutions per minute, and is strong and substantial in every respect and the best machine in the market for the purpose.

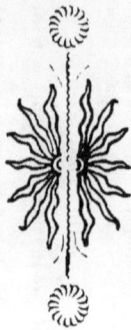

ALEXANDER W. WINTER,

... PROCESSES FOR ...

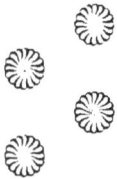

Refining, Deodorizing, Bleaching Lards, Tallows, Oils and Greases; also for Oleomargarine Oil and Oleomargarine Butter,

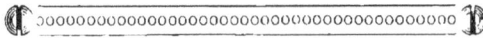

A SPECIALTY.

Plants fitted up and start= ed. Competent men fur= nished for all departments.

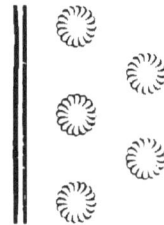

Plans furnished and Machinery supplied.

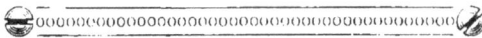

Advice given on any of the above branches.

Twenty=five years' practical experience.

Correspondence solicited.

Office and Laboratory, 5747 Dearborn Street,
CHICAGO.

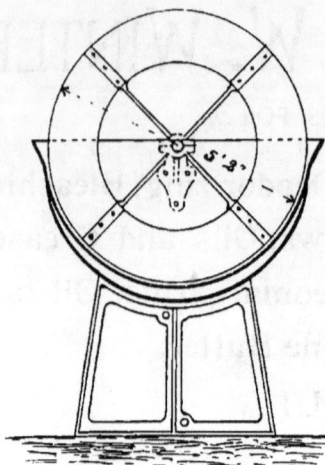

LARD COOLER
MURRAY IRON WORKS CO.
BURLINGTON, IOWA.

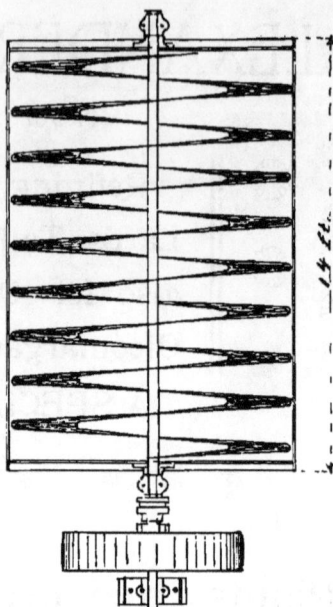

This is without doubt the best Lard Cooler that has ever been offered to the Trade.

THE

MURRAY

IRON

WORKS

CO.,

BURLINGTON,

IOWA.

It consists of a double jacket and a large spiral agitator.

It possesses a very decided advantage over all other Coolers made, in that, instead of the lard being in a deep tank where the air can not reach it, it is in a shallow tank, thus being exposed to the cooling action of the air on all sides, on account of the lard clinging to the spiral agitator while revolving.

It does its work much more rapidly than any other machine and acts at the same time as an absolute preventive of lumpy lard.

It is quickly and easily cleaned by allowing the water in the jacket to pass off and allowing steam to enter.

It is made of boiler iron and will last forever.

Detailed information with prices on application.

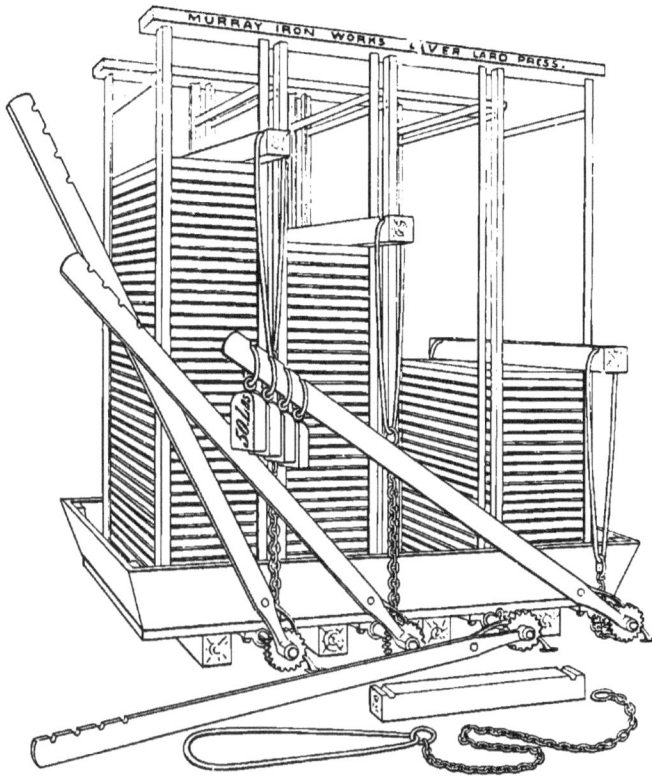

LEVER LARD PRESS

... MANUFACTURED BY THE ...

MURRAY IRON WORKS CO.,

Burlington, Iowa.

We beg to call the special attention of the Trade to this Press. We claim for it the following

⇒▷ UNUSUAL ADVANTAGES ◁⇐

First.   It is **automatic**, requiring no pumps or steam power.

Second.   It makes a better oil than any other press on the market, on account of the pressure being self-acting and **not forced.**

Third.   As this press comes four to a set, one man can easily handle it, filling two of the sets with five tierces each, and emptying the other two the same day and preparing them for filling the next day.
It possesses many other advantages which can not be enumerated here.

It is now used by all the large Packers in Chicago.

FULL PARTICULARS ON APPLICATION.

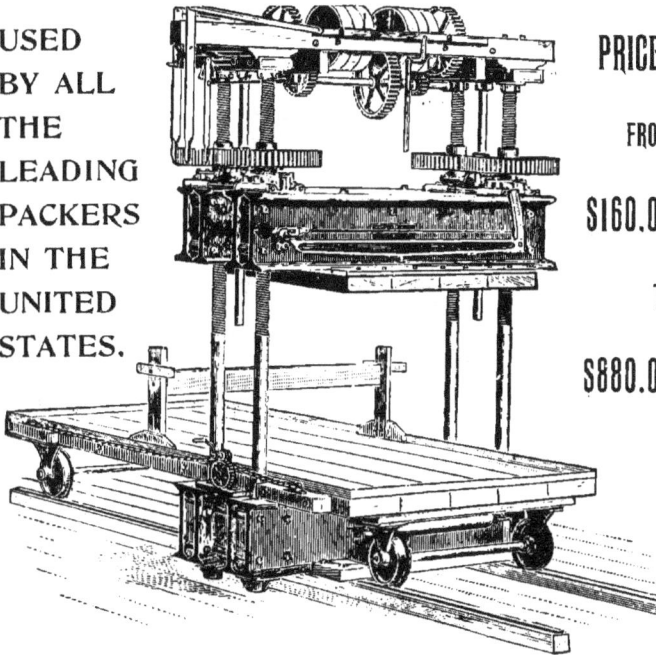

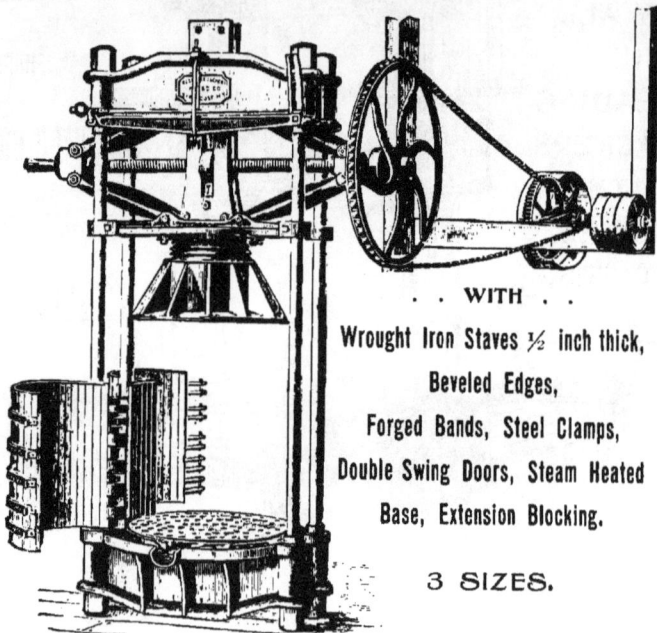

Errata

PAGE 64

The line " THE JOHNSON FILTER PRESS " should be under the engraving.

PAGE 106

PAGE 116

This cut, representing an OLEOMARGARINE PRESS, is the illustration that is referred to in the last two lines of page 106. The same press is referred to on page 116, in the last paragraph on the page.

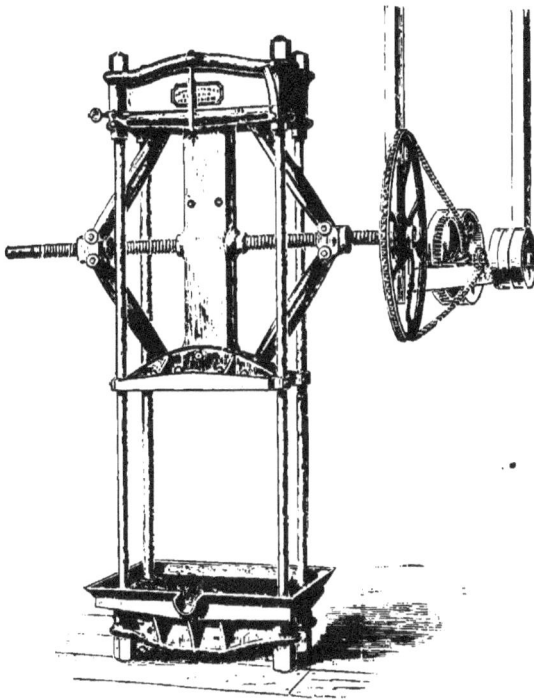

Recipe No. 1

Pure Kettle Lard

RECIPE NO. 1
PURE KETTLE LARD

In order to make a PURE KETTLE LARD, the leaf lard of the hog is taken and hashed, and from the hasher it is run into a jacket kettle, which should be provided with an agitator.

It is then heated and cooked for about SIX HOURS, at a temperature of 240 degrees Fahrenheit, the agitator continually turning the stock.

It is then allowed to settle and is run off into packages.

While cooking this stock, use say 20 lbs. of salt to a batch of 5,000 lbs. of leaf lard, for settling purposes.

The remaining stock, after the pure kettle lard has run off, is either put into the tanks for prime steam, or it can be pressed and the cracklings sold for feeding hogs; but it is preferable and best to take the whole mess and put it into the prime steam tank.

Recipe No. 2

Kettle Rendered Lard

RECIPE NO. 2

KETTLE RENDERED LARD

A fine kettle rendered lard is made by using

      20 lbs. Leaf Lard
      12 lbs. Lard-stearine
      68 lbs. Back Fat
     100 lbs. Kettle Rendered Lard.

Cook four hours at a temperature of 260 degrees Fahrenheit. Let the stock cook two hours, then add ten pounds of salt. Then cook for two hours longer, add ten pounds more salt and allow all to settle for half an hour. Then draw into a settling tank and allow it to settle for one hour. It is then ready for drawing into packages. The agitator in the kettle should run at the rate of about thirty revolutions a minute. The lard should be drawn for tins at about 200 degrees Fahrenheit and for tierces at from 100 to 110 degrees Fahrenheit.

Recipe No. 3

Prime Steam Lard

RECIPE NO. 3
PRIME STEAM LARD

In order to make a choice PRIME STEAM LARD, the stock should be cooked immediately.   Laying it over and holding it until you have enough for a full tank, always makes the lard of an inferior standard.   But if the tanks are in readiness immediately after the killing and the stock is placed in them at once, it will make a fine white lard.

Prime steam lard should be cooked for about eight hours, under a steam pressure of 60 lbs.

I would recommend cooking it. for about TWO hours at the start, with plenty of water.   Then allow it to settle and draw the water off; then put in fresh water and finish cooking.

Of course, in cooking this stock, it is important to always have the pet cocks on the top of the tank blowing off, so as to allow the gases to escape.

Have your tanks so arranged that the water will go in from the bottom and not from the top, as I have seen it often done. The water-pipes being so arranged that it flows in from the bottom, it will allow you to raise the lard up to the cocks and draw it off to the last particle.   The water must be let in slowly.

After all of the lard is off. the drop-door is let fall and the whole mess dropped into a tank, where it is carefully skimmed.

Then the water is run off, and the remaining stock pressed in a tankage press, such as is made by the Boomer & Boschert Press Co., Syracuse, N. Y., an engraving of which is shown on opposite page.

The tankage is then taken to the drier and fertilizer made out of it.

TANKAGE PRESS
WORKED BY HAND

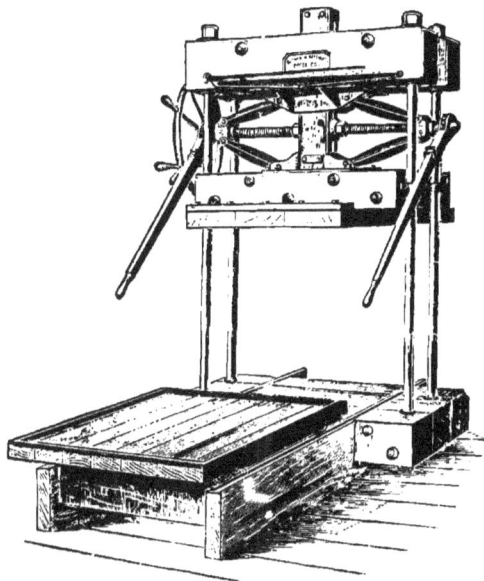

This style of platform is often used by the smaller packers requiring a limited capacity. Power can be attached to any size at a cost of from $40 to $45

Recipe No. 4

Choice Family Lard

RECIPE NO. 4
CHOICE FAMILY LARD

This is a grade of lard that is generally made out of

    40 lbs. Lard
    20 lbs. Tallow
    20 lbs. Cotton Oil
    20 lbs. Off Lard
    ──────
    100 lbs. CHOICE FAMILY LARD

Recipe No. 5

Cottoline

RECIPE NO. 5
COTTOLINE

COTTOLINE is made out of cotton oil and oleo-stearine in the following proportions:

                60 lbs. Cotton Oil
                40 lbs. Oleo-stearine
               100 lbs. COTTOLINE.

To make a good cottoline, this stock is never bleached or refined, but should have a nice grain and be of a yellow color.

It should not be heated too highly. I have always found that it was best flavored when heated at a temperature of not more than 180 degrees Fahrenheit.

It is used by bakers and is in growing demand.

After it is heated to 180 degrees Fahrenheit, put the blower on.

Blow well until all is dissolved and thoroughly mixed.

No fuller's earth or other refining stock must be used.

After it is all well mixed and properly heated, start the pump going, and pump the cottoline through a filter.

Then pass it over the roller into the agitator and finally draw into tierces.

Recipe No. 6

Lard Compound

RECIPE NO. 6
LARD COMPOUND

LARD COMPOUND is made out of

60 lbs. Cotton Oil
20 lbs. Deodorized Hog Grease
10 lbs. Tallow
10 lbs. Oleo-stearine
100 lbs. LARD COMPOUND.

Recipe No. 7

Silver Leaf Lard

RECIPE NO. 7

SILVER LEAF LARD

This grade of lard may be made out of prime steam lard; the proportions are :

> 80 lbs. Prime Steam Lard
> 20 lbs. Lard-stearine
> 100 lbs. SILVER LEAF LARD.

During the months of June, July and August, fully 25 to 30 per cent lard-stearine is used. When the cooler weather sets in and all through the winter months, no lard-stearine is used.

This grade of lard, if properly refined, makes a beautiful pure-white lard and sells rapidly.

It is packed in tins of 3, 5, 10, 20 and 50 lbs.; also in all sizes of wooden packages and tierces.

In making this grade of lard, I would suggest that in tanking the prime steam lard for the purpose of manufacturing silver leaf lard one should arrange it so as to use a considerable quantity of back fat in this grade.

Recipe No. 8

imitation Steam Lard

41

RECIPE NO. 8

IMITATION STEAM LARD

IMITATION STEAM LARD is made out of

> 60 lbs. Lard
> 40 lbs. Tallow
> 100 lbs. IMITATION STEAM LARD.

The 60 per cent of lard trimmings and the 40 per cent of tallow trimmings, are put into the lard tanks, and with it, if possible, some of the remaining stock from kettle-lard.

It is then cooked and handled the same as the prime steam lard.

I have tanked lard on this formula and cooked it well, so that it had precisely the same flavor as a pure prime steam, and could pass for a steam lard.

Recipe No. 9

Cuba Lard

43

RECIPE NO. 9

CUBA LARD

My experience with Cuba lard has been that in shipping to Cuba, a great deal depends on the party to whom the lard is shipped.

Some of the dealers in Cuba want a strictly prime steam lard.   This is packed in tins of different sizes.

Then again, some trade wants a lard that is made somewhat like our imitation steam lard.

Then again, some want it with 40 per cent water.

I have found it a difficult trade to satisfy. unless it is in the supply of pure steam lard.

The following are some of the formulas I have used when manufacturing Cuba lard for a large packing house:

                    30 lbs. Lard
                    10 lbs. White Deodorized Grease
                    40 lbs. Tallow
                    20 lbs. Cotton Oil
                   100 lbs. Cuba Lard.

30 lbs. Lard
10 lbs. White Deodorized Grease
40 lbs Tallow
20 lbs. Jawbone Stock
100 lbs. Cuba Lard.

60 lbs. Tallow
25 lbs. White Deodorized Grease
15 lbs. Cotton Oil
100 lbs. Cuba Lard.
To this add 20 per cent Water

            75 lbs. Tallow
            25 lbs. White Deodorized Grease
           100 lbs. Cuba Lard.

Recipe No. 10

Watered Lard

RECIPE NO. 10
WATERED LARD

In order to make a WATERED LARD, you take say one barrel of the best "plasterer's lime;" this you stock with about five or six barrels of water.

Let your man stir the lime well and get it thoroughly dissolved, then allow it to settle and use the liquor; this will be of a clear blue color.

Now to use it you take such percentage as you desire to carry, and when the lard is in the agitator, you let the water run in slowly, allowing the agitator to work steadily for one hour after the water is in, also while the water is running into this lard. Let the agitator continue in motion until all of the lard is drawn off, not drawing off any lard, however, before you have made sure that all the water has been taken up and is thoroughly mixed with the lard.

Recipe No. 11

Processes for Refining Lard

RECIPE NO. 11
PROCESSES FOR REFINING LARD

Run the lard to be refined into a jacket kettle

A. REFINING SILVER LEAF LARD

Heat up to 190 degrees Fahrenheit. Start the blower going and, when all is melted, put in about 3 per cent fuller's earth and let the blower mix it well.

When the earth is in the lard, and the blower has run, say four or five minutes, start your pump and pump through the filter. The lard should come out as clear as distilled water.

Let the blower work all the time you are pumping, so as not to let the fuller's earth settle.

B. REFINING CHOICE FAMILY LARD

Put your ingredients into the jacket tank and heat to about 215 to 220 degrees Fahrenheit; then add about 7 per cent fuller's earth, and let it be well blown by the blower.

When it is well mixed and agitated, start the pump and run the lard through the filter into the receiver; then over the roller into the agitator, and then pack in such packages as you desire.

C. REFINING LARD COMPOUND

This operation is done by means of the recipe relating to the refining of Choice Family Lard, the only difference being that you may be obliged to use a little more fuller's earth than on the Choice Family Lard.

Recipe No. 12

Process for Bleaching Lards, Oils
Tallows and Greases

RECIPE NO. 12
PROCESS FOR BLEACHING LARDS, OILS
TALLOWS AND GREASES

When it is desired to bleach lards, oils, tallows and greases. the products are put into jacket tanks and heated to above 215 degrees Fahrenheit, and fuller's earth is added until the desired color is obtained.

The process for treating these ingredients will be found fully explained in the preceding recipes.

Recipe No. 13

Process for Deodorizing Lards, Oils
Tallows and Greases

RECIPE NO. 13
PROCESS FOR DEODORIZING LARDS. OILS
TALLOWS AND GREASES

Here is undoubtedly the best deodorizing process, and it is known only to a very few.

For twenty barrels of grease or oil take four pounds of permanganate of potash, with three pounds of bichromate of potash and one pound of sal soda.

Dissolve together in the chemical tank, in five barrels of water, the bichromate of potash and the soda; then put in the permanganate of potash and dissolve that. Then allow this solution to run into the grease.

Turn on the air and mix the chemical solution and the grease or oil; then add sulphuric acid of 66 degrees Beaume, diluted with half water. Add this acid in the proportion of one quart clear acid to each pound of the chemicals.

When the reaction takes place and the grease turns to a green color, turn on steam in addition to the air, and allow the air to continue for five minutes; then shut off the air and bring to a lively boil.

When boiled, shut off steam and allow to settle; it will take ten to twenty minutes. Then draw off the chemical water and spray with a hose thoroughly, using clear water. Allow it to settle and draw off this water. Then make a mixture of one-half pound sal soda in one tierce of water and pour it into the washing tank.

Run the bleached grease into this and boil two hours and then allow the water to settle.

This is for poor grades of stock that you want deodorized.

In treating any quantity of grease or oil it will only be necessary to change the quantity of the chemicals in the same proportion.

To deodorize white grease or smothered hog grease from all bad odor, a one-pound mixture is sufficient for each barrel. Use, in that case, the following mixture:

> One-half lb. Permanganate of Potash
> Three-eighths lb. Bichromate of Potash
> One-eighth lb. Sal Soda
>
> Total, One lb. Chemicals.

In using acid, it will be sufficient to use one quart of pure sulphuric acid to each pound of chemicals used as above, diluting the acid one-half with water, always figuring on the addition of pure acid; then dilute.

Just at this point I think a few words regarding the use and manipulation of smothered hogs, or hogs that have died of disease, may be in order. It may not be known to the smaller packers in the smaller towns to what an extent such animals are used in the manufacture of the cheaper grades of lard. In the smaller towns and neighborhoods such animals are generally buried. They can generally be obtained from the farmers for hauling them away. It is a very simple matter to render them in a tank, the whole carcass being thrown in and thoroughly boiled. After boiling, allow it to settle thoroughly. Skim off the lard and treat it as directed in Recipe No. 13, and the result will be a beautifully clear, white and odorless lard. When it is considered that a three hundred pound hog, treated as above shown, will yield about 130 pounds of lard that will sell readily for six cents per pound, it will be evident that this is a branch of the business that is well worth looking into. The residue of the animal may be used for fertilizer, as directed in Recipes Nos. 31, 32 and 33. Great caution must be exercised in handling such animals. I have seen them lying on the platforms at the Union Stock Yards, Chicago, swollen to twice their natural size and burst open. They should ALWAYS be handled with hooks or with gloves. If handled with naked hands on which there is the slightest scratch or sore, blood poisoning is almost sure to follow and cause most serious trouble. It will be seen from the above that the careful manipulation of such animals by CAREFUL PEOPLE will bring good returns to many who have heretofore given no attention to anything of the kind. Fats of any other animals than hogs may be thoroughly deodorized by the use of Recipe No. 13, pressed by a lever press such as is manufactured by the Murray Iron Works of Burlington, Iowa, and the oil used for lubricating purposes, and the stearine sold to soap manufacturers or used in ANY MIXTURE or for ANY PURPOSE that the manipulator may desire.

A tank to treat 20 tierces should be 4 ft. in diameter at the bottom, 7 ft. diameter at the top and 10 ft. high. The staves, 2 inches thick, to be all of clear, kiln-dried pine, bottom dished to center one inch; the tank should have 9 hoops, each with clamps of round iron. Estimated cost: $75.00.

A TEST OF THE ABOVE RECIPE

To make a small test of this most valuable recipe, take a 4-ounce bottle, fill it quarter full with the stock to be tested; add one-third size of bottle of the chemicals mixed in above proportions; add a little sulphuric acid; shake it well until the mixture assumes a light color, then add a little live steam, using a small hose or pipe for the purpose; then boil for thirty seconds. The bottle will not break if it is a regular 4-ounce bottle. After this, allow the matter to settle. This will at once show whether the grease will pay for handling it.

A FEW SPECIAL POINTS CONCERNING RECIPE No. 13

Be sure to use oil of vitriol of 66 degrees Beaume, and mix it in one half water.

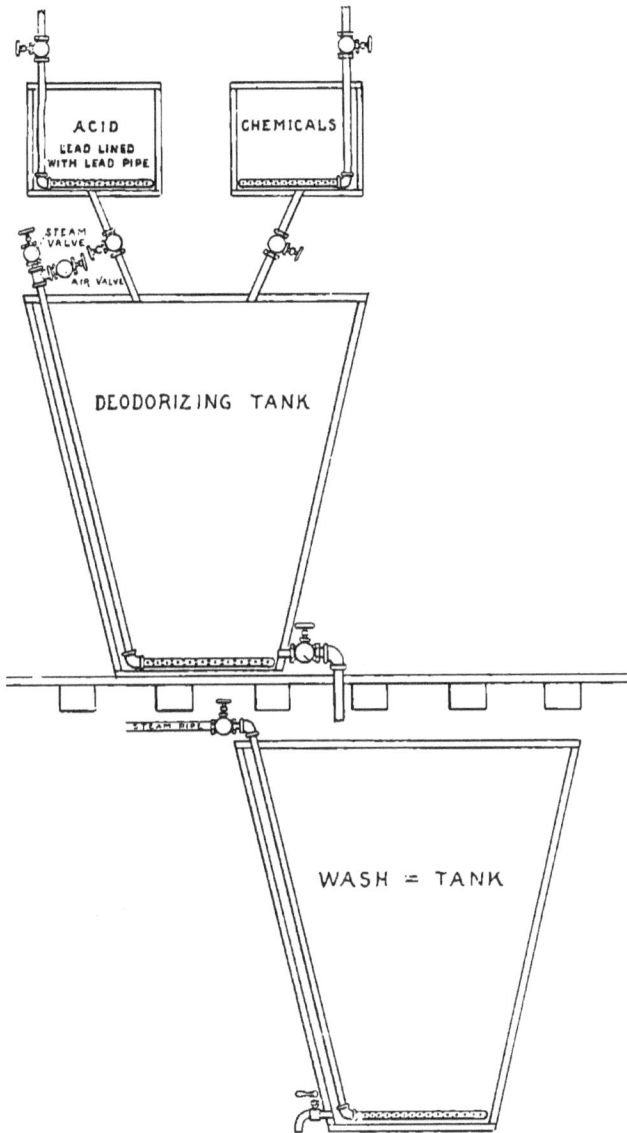

ACID
LEAD LINED
WITH LEAD PIPE

CHEMICALS

STEAM VALVE

AIR VALVE

DEODORIZING TANK

STEAM PIPE

WASH = TANK

In starting to deodorize do not use any steam, as the stock, if steamed out of the tierces, will be heated, and the chemicals will keep it at the proper heat.

The deodorizing tank is to be of wood, with a lead pipe for introducing steam, and a connection at the top, as shown in the drawing, for introducing air at the bottom.   Be sure to see that no iron connections are used in this tank; have only regular fittings FOR ACID USE.

The first step, to start with, is to steam the stock to be used out of the tierces into the deodorizing tank.   After it is in the tank, let it settle and draw off the water from the bottom. Put the blower on and allow air to enter; then let the chemicals run in; the stock will then turn a very black color.   Then run in the acid and let the reaction take place.   Keep the blower going until the stock changes color; it will soon do so, becoming lighter and lighter.   This will take about half an hour; then add open steam.   Keep boiling, with the blower and open steam on, until the stock comes to a boil; then shut off the blower, but let the open steam continue.   Boil the stock for about five or ten minutes; then allow it to settle and draw off the water saturated with chemicals.   Fresh water is then added with the hose in a thorough spray.   No blowing or boiling is necessary during this operation. Allow the stock to settle; draw off the water and repeat.   Then run the stock into the wash tank and boil with open steam.   Be sure to have the sal soda, spoken of above, in this tank and boil hard.

Have two small tanks above the deodorizing tanks, the acid tank to hold two barrels and the chemical tank five barrels; the acid tank must be lined with lead.   The arrangement of tanks can be seen at a glance by referring to the full-page engraving on the preceding page.

Recipe No. 14

Process for Clarifying Lards, Oils
Tallows and Greases

RECIPE NO. 14.
PROCESS FOR CLARIFYING LARDS, OILS
TALLOWS AND GREASES.

To clarify lards, oils, tallows and grease, the heat in the jacket kettle must reach 230 degrees Fahrenheit; let the blower agitate the stock for two hours at that temperature.

Then pump through the filter and let the stock cool in the receiver; draw off when cooled.

Never draw oil into barrels when it is hot or even simply warm. Let it be well chilled before drawing; otherwise your oil will be cloudy.

Suggestions

As to Machinery needed for the Proper
Working of the Preceding
Processes

SUGGESTIONS
AS TO MACHINERY NEEDED FOR
THE PROPER WORKING OF
THE PRECEDING PROCESSES

The machinery required for an ordinary lard, oil and grease refinery is to be composed of :

1ST. A JACKET KETTLE TO HOLD 10,000 LBS. I suggest a jacket kettle of this size for this reason: In fitting up a plant it is best to put in a kettle of this size so as not to be crowded for space. In a 10,000-lb. jacket kettle you may run as little as you choose; and then, again, should you get a large order you can run it all on the same day.   With a 10,000-lb. plant you can, if pushed, put through 20,000 lbs. in ten hours.   My experience has been that in nine cases out of ten, where any smaller plants were put in, I was called upon to take them out and replace them by 10,000-lb. plants.   It costs no more to run a batch of 10,000 lbs. than it would to run 3,000 lbs.; so that it is practically CHEAPER to put in a large plant than a small one.   And the first requirement for a 10,000-lb. plant is a 10,000-lb. jacket kettle.   On the opposite page will be found an engraving of a 10,000-lb. kettle with all necessary fittings.

2D. ONE BLOWER-PUMP ENGINE. As there are several of these pumps on the market, be sure, when ordering yours, to have it well understood that it will pump against a 100-lb. pressure.   I have found the pump made by the Wheeler & Tappan Company, Chicago, the best for this purpose.

3D. ONE FILTER OF 36 PLATES, 24 INCHES IN DIAMETER, WITH COCKS ON EACH PLATE.

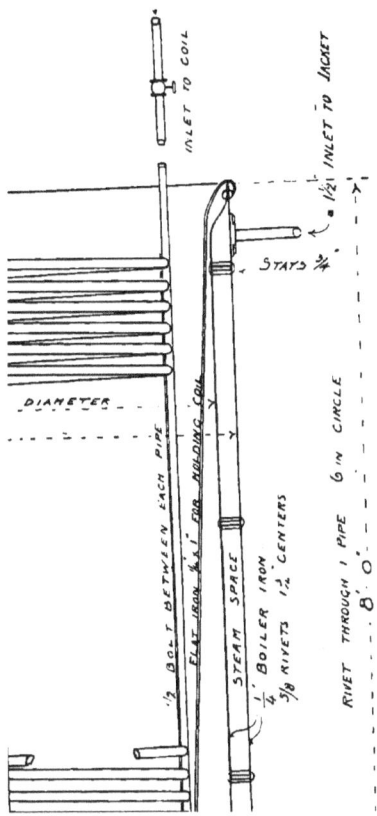

INLET TO COIL

1¼" INLET TO JACKET

STAYS ¾"

DIAMETER

½ BOLT BETWEEN EACH PIPE

FLAT IRON ¾ × 1" FOR HOLDING COIL

STEAM SPACE

¼" BOILER IRON

5/8 RIVETS 1½ CENTERS

RIVET THROUGH 1 PIPE   6 IN CIRCLE

8' 0'

FILTRATION AND THE FILTER PRESS

Before going into the details of the construction and description of working filter presses, I will give an outline description of a few methods of separating solid from liquid which were in general use before the introduction of the filter press, for the purpose of making a comparison with the filter press.

FILTRATION, as a part of the refining process, demands serious consideration. No process of refining oils, lard, tallow or greases is perfect so long as the slightest trace of solid impurities is present in them (at the temperature necessary for filtration). Various methods have been adopted to separate the solid impurities from the liquid in which it is contained. The first I will mention is the

SETTLING TANK, usually a large tank into which the oil is placed and in which the solid particles are intended to precipitate by gravitation; some of these solid particles, being of the same specific gravity as the oil, do not precipitate, but remain suspended in the oil indefinitely; in some cases months are lost in this method of settling out the solid impurities, after which time the work is only imperfectly done.

THE GRAVITATION FILTER, generally a wooden frame with a filter cloth stretched over it and secured at the four corners so as to form a depression in the middle, into which is put the material to be filtered; the filtrate (or portion which passes through the cloth) is caught in a vessel placed under the filter. Now this method, although very simple, has many objections; among them is the great amount of room necessary to filter large quantities of material; the operation is necessarily very slow, and the residue remaining in the filter is generally a pulpy mass, which requires rehandling if it is desired to recover the oil remaining in it; consequently there is great loss of room, time and material when filtering by this method. Great improvements have been made in machinery for the separation of solid from liquid, which have resulted in producing the modern filter press.

Advantages Gained by the Filter Press over Old Time Methods of Separating Solids from Liquids

1st. Economy of Space. The method adopted of distributing the filtering surface in the filter press secures an enormous filtering area within a comparatively small space.

2d. Saving of Time. What formerly took months to accomplish in the settling tank can now be done in an hour with the filter press.

3d. Quality of Work Done. All solid impurities, no matter what their size or specific gravity may be, are completely removed from the liquid.

4th. Quantity of Work Done. The material to be filtered is forced through the filter press under high pressure; consequently, large quantities can be filtered in a very short time.

5th. Complete Separation of the Oil from the Cake, as in the case of decolorizing oils, lards and greases with fuller's earth. The earth during filtration is collected in the form of compact cakes containing some of the oil or grease, which can be removed completely by steaming the cake before taking it from the filter press, no handling afterward being necessary.

DESCRIPTION OF THE FILTER PRESS

Since the introduction of the filter press, all other modes for separating and collecting precipitates from liquids have become obsolete. The filter press consists of a series of round or square plates, made of cast iron,

lead, hard wood or other suitable material, having projecting lugs, so that they can be supported in a press
frame, in juxtaposition, face to face, and screwed up
tightly between the head and follower of the press. The
plates are concave on each side, while the projecting,
truly-faced rims maintain the plate surfaces at distances
corresponding to the depth of two rims. Faced rings
can be inserted between the rims of two plates, to in-
crease the distance between their surfaces. The
plates, provided with channels communicating with
outlets at the bottom, are covered with suitable filtering
cloth. Thus the spaces between the cloth-lined plates
form chambers, into which the semi-fluid material to
be filtered is forced under pressure. A passage, also
lined with cloth, is formed through each plate, so that
there is communication between all the filtering chambers. A pair of cloths are used to cover each side of a
plate, sewed together round a center-hole, corresponding
to the opening in the plate. It is obvious that on fold-
ing one cloth, passing it through the hole in the plate,
and then opening it out, both surfaces of the latter will
be covered. The hooks on the plates, to which the
filtering cloth is fastened, are movable by means of
screw spindles, so that slackness of the filters can be
taken up in a radial direction, thus insuring tight joints
between the plates. The material for the filters, which
must combine strength, durability and closeness of
texture, is specially manufactured and called "lamb-
skin." When the solution to be filtered is forced into
the chambers of the press, the liquid is driven through
the cloth, and flows away through the outlets at the

bottom of the plates, while the solid matter is arrested in the chambers. Finally, when the solid matter fills every chamber completely, the operation of charging is suspended. This is indicated by the filtrate ceasing to flow from the outlets of the plates at the maximum pressure, say 150 pounds per square inch, for which the press is designed. Now the press is unscrewed, the plates are separated, and, without removing the filters, the chambers are emptied, their contents being in the form of solid cakes with more or less moisture, according to the character of the precipitate and the pressure in charging. The latter is indicated by a pressure-gauge. It does not take more than one minute to unload each chamber.

These machines are also constructed with square plates, and, in some special cases, arranged for using filtering paper instead of cloth as the filtering medium.

To do first-class work economically, it is necessary to be provided with first-class apparatus.

I have used various machines and appliances for filtering oils, greases, lard, etc., but the above described filter press has always given me such thorough satisfaction that I strongly recommend its use to those who adopt any of my various processes requiring filtration. Personally, I have always selected this machine for my various filtering operations.

4TH. ONE DUPLEX PUMP, 4 x 6 x 4. I would recommend Wheeler & Tappan's style. I have used it and found it to give good results.

5TH. ONE IRON RECEIVER, CAPACITY 10,000 LBS. This is to be placed directly under the filter, so as to catch the stock that is pumped through the filter.

6TH. ONE CYLINDER ROLLER, 9 FEET LONG AND 4 FEET IN DIAMETER. I would recommend the cylinder roller made by the Wheeler & Tappan Company, as it is of the greatest importance to have a good cylinder, cast smooth and solid. All the lard runs over this cylinder and is cooled off rapidly. This appliance is also of the greatest importance in amalgamating the different ingredients so that they are not apt to separate in hot weather. From the cylinder the lard will drop into

7TH. A BOX, under which a pump is placed, and from this box it is pumped into

8TH. THE LARD COOLER, made by the Murray Iron Works Company, of Burlington, Iowa, who have made most of the agitators in use.

The reason for pumping the stock into the cooler and not letting it drop direct from the cylinder roller into it, is that by pumping it we get rid of all lumps, and have only a smooth lard This process has been arrived at after spending thousands of dollars in experiments to find out how to get rid of lumpy lard.

From the agitator the lard is run into the different packages. scales being placed on an adjustable platform. The packages to be filled are placed on the scales, and when filled are set aside to cool.

When fitting up a refinery or packing house, it is all important to have all piping, iron and brass fittings, valves, steam fittings, etc., the best that can be had.   The goods supplied by the Crane Company can always be depended on.

Recipe No. 15

How to Pack Lard

63

RECIPE NO. 15

HOW TO PACK LARD

A great many refiners find, after packing their lard from the agitator in tubs and other packages, that, when they examine it the next morning, it has caved in in the middle and is badly cracked. This has caused them considerable trouble.

This inconvenience can be remedied by allowing the lard to cool slowly.   When drawing the lard from the agitator it is usually placed in a freezing temperature, and this, as a rule, will cause the lard to crack and sink down in the middle.

Lard should be drawn off thick and allowed to cool in a temperature of about 36 degrees Fahrenheit.

SIZES OF PACKAGES USED

For the United States the packages in general use are:
Tierces
Buckets
Tubs
Tins
and Fancy Tubs Grained.

The tins are termed
3-lb. Tins
5-lb. Tins
10-lb. Tins
20-lb. Tins
50-lb. Tins.

In summer a summer cover is put on over them with a crimp-ing machine, so that they can be shipped to hot climates and not leak.

This crimping machine is most important and all those who do any shipping of lard should have one, as by its operation the packages are made air tight.   No solder is used; the package is crimped air-tight and the cover easily removed.

Next come the ASH TUBS.   Ash tubs are sold in assorted sizes by the car lot; they generally run in the following sizes:

10 lbs.	50 lbs.
15 lbs.	55 lbs.
20 lbs.	60 lbs.
25 lbs.	80 lbs.
30 lbs.	Very few 80-lb. Tubs
35 lbs.	are now used.

Next come what are called FANCY TUBS.   These are consid-ered very pretty packages.   They run in all sizes from 10 lbs. to 80 lbs.

These are the principal small packages used.

TIERCES averaging about 340 lbs. net, BARRELS of 200 lbs. and HALF-BARRELS of 125 lbs. are also used to a very large ex-tent.

CABLES VERSUS HOOPS

Cable Ware, having welded wire hoops indented into the wood at intervals, makes it impossible for the hoops to drop off, no matter what the conditions may be. The strength of the wire hoop is three times as great as that of the flat hoop, and, being made of steel, the indentations act as a spring so that the hoop contracts or expands in accordance with the condition of the wood in the pail or tub, and makes breakage impossible. The most durable ware made, as it cannot burst the hoops like common ware, neither can the hoops drop off under any circumstances or in any climate, however dry it may be; and in addition to all this, it has three times the strength of common ware. The Cable Bound Packages are made by Mann Brothers, Chicago.

Recipe No. 16

How to put a Crimp on Lard to Imitate
a Pure Kettle Leaf Lard

73

RECIPE NO. 16
HOW TO PUT A CRIMP ON LARD
TO IMITATE A PURE
KETTLE LEAF LARD

This has been experimented upon at a great expense of time and money. Indeed, it has been extremely difficult to obtain a regular, uniform result, but it has been finally reached and here is the process in full.

We all know that a pure kettle lard, if properly drawn, has a rough top to it, while all other lards are smooth-topped. We have discovered how a prime steam lard can be brought up to the same condition. The process is very simple.

When making a pure lard like silver leaf, in order to make it appear like a pure kettle leaf lard you must draw it direct from the receiver. It must not be cooled, but run into the packages at about 160 degrees Fahrenheit. Then you spread the packages well, so that plenty of air may pass between them and allow the lard to cool as quickly as possible.

It must not be moved or jarred. It must be left perfectly quiet and cooled quickly; it will then be found white, firm and beautiful, and will have the desired ROUGH TOP.

I would recommend, when making this grade of lard, and in case you make your own steam lard, that you should always mix as much back fat as you can spare with your steam lard. This will make this brand a highly flavored lard, and you can always command for it a high price and brand it "Pure Lard," with a guarantee.

Just here I would make a suggestion as to the name to be chosen for this imitation of pure leaf lard. It will be found highly advantageous to work into the name the word "leaf," as the consumer will always have greater confidence in a brand that is called "leaf." "Silver Leaf," "Gold Leaf," "Maple Leaf," are all good names, as they convey to the consumer the idea they are getting LEAF LARD, and, therefore, something that is certainly pure. "A WORD TO THE WISE IS SUFFICIENT."

Recipe No. 17

Temperature at which Lard should be Pumped through the Filter

RECIPE NO. 17
TEMPERATURE AT WHICH LARD
SHOULD BE PUMPED
THROUGH THE FILTER

The temperature is

For Lard Compound, 200 to 210 degrees Fahrenheit
For Choice Family Lard, the same
For Silver Leaf Lard, about 180 degrees Fahrenheit

Recipe No. 18

How to Fit up a Filter so that it can be
Readily Cleaned without the Loss
of a Particle of Lard

RECIPE NO. 18

HOW TO FIT UP A FILTER

SO THAT IT CAN BE READILY CLEANED

WITHOUT THE LOSS OF A

PARTICLE OF LARD

In the first place, the filter should be set on blocks just high enough to allow the trough to be 4 inches higher than the refining kettle. This kettle should be set up through the floor about one foot. The tank, as seen in the diagram on opposite page, will be about one foot up. The filter is on blocks, so as to be a little higher than the tank. The reason for this is that, when you start pumping through the filter, at first the stock will be a little "off" color. This portion of the stock must not, of course, be allowed into the receiver, but must run back into the refining tank until the color is right. The trough of the filter must be so arranged that when you first start filtering, the stock will run from the trough into the refining tank. When the stock is clear and of the right color, a cock is shut off, and it runs into the receiver under the filter.

Here is a diagram of the connections. One cock is close to

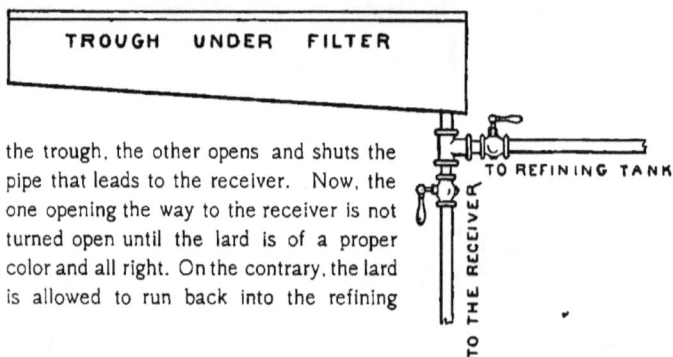

TROUGH   UNDER   FILTER

TO REFINING TANK

TO THE RECEIVER

the trough, the other opens and shuts the pipe that leads to the receiver. Now, the one opening the way to the receiver is not turned open until the lard is of a proper color and all right. On the contrary, the lard is allowed to run back into the refining

kettle or tank until it is satisfactory; and if it should be too long in assuming the proper color, all you have to do is to add a little more fuller's earth. By the above arrangement it is never necessary to have any bad or off color lard, for you can keep on refining it until the color comes out right; when it is finally of the proper color, you turn OFF the cock that connects the trough with the tank, and turn on the cock that connects with the receiver.

The filter must be so arranged that you can pump through, first the refined lard, then the air, then the steam, and to do this you rig up your filter and pump as shown by the engraving below.

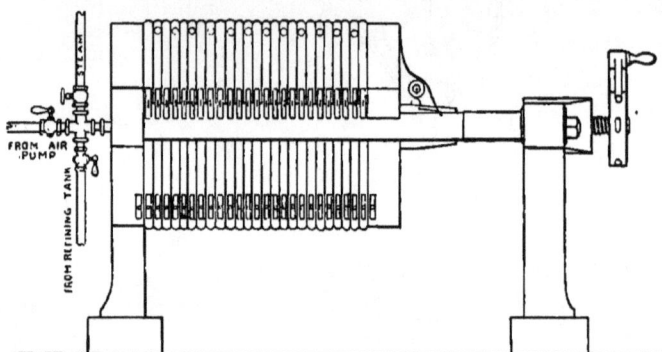

This diagram shows two cocks, besides one valve for steam. Use pipe no smaller than one and one-half inch in diameter. The down pipe is the one coming from the refining kettle or tank, and the lard is pumped from the bottom up through the filter. When the tank is empty the pump is stopped and this cock is turned off. Of course the filter will then be full of lard. Now to save this you open the air-cock, start your air pump and pump until all the lard is out of the filter; this will take say ten to fifteen minutes. When no more lard comes with the air blower, you turn this cock off and open your steam. But be sure before opening the steam to change the cocks on the trough, for if you don't do so water will get mixed with the lard. Have your trough provided with a 2-inch hole at each end. When pumping through the filter close the one end and let the stock run into the receiver. When you start steaming shut this off and open the other end, to which a pipe is attached going through the floor; a barrel is to be placed underneath to catch the water and lard.

After the steam has done its work—and it must be kept on until no more lard is in the filter— nothing but the fuller's earth being left in the filter, then the steam is shut off, the filter opened and the fuller's earth drops out by shaking the cloths; a wooden scraper is used to clean what little of it is left on the cloths. The earth is of no value after being steamed. The cloths can be used three or four times. It is well to have two or three sets of cloths and always to use a clean set whenever making a change of formula. For instance, a lard compound having just been run through it will not do to put a silver leaf through the same cloths. But if you are running two or three runs of compound in succession, it is all right to use the same set of cloths, provided, of course, that they are properly cleaned with steam after each run and the old fuller's earth shaken out.

All pipes should be so arranged as to have drain cocks. Always be sure to drain your pipes; otherwise you will soon be blocked. Have no L's put in, but T's at all turns, with plugs, so that if you do get blocked, you can clear your pipes without having to take them all down. By fitting up the filter as explained herein there should not be one particle of loss of stock, since the steam should be kept on until there is no more grease at all mixed with the fuller's earth.

Recipe No. 19

At what Temperature Lard should go over the Roller

RECIPE NO. 19
AT WHAT TEMPERATURE LARD
SHOULD GO
OVER THE ROLLER

Lard should go over the roller at a temperature of 120 degrees Fahrenheit, but if you are rushed, it may go over much hotter. Of course the hotter it goes over the more cold water you will have to use.

A good way to do, if time allows, is to run your lard in the afternoon and to leave it in the receiver over night, and the next morning run it over the roller. By so doing you will save a great deal of water. Be sure, in leaving the lard over night, that it does not grow too cold so that it will be stiff in the morning, for it must remain in a liquid state, so that it will run out of the receiver readily.

In large packing houses they nave not the time to hold their lard, but refine it all day and run it over the rollers continuously; but then they have ice-machines and use brine for cooling the roller. In smaller packing houses it is better to hold it over night if you can.

Recipe No. 20

At what Temperature Water should go into the Roller

RECIPE NO. 20
AT WHAT TEMPERATURE
WATER SHOULD GO INTO
THE ROLLER

The water in the roller should be at least 36 degrees Fahrenheit.   Now, to obtain this temperature in summer if you have no brine, put a large tank on the floor above the roller; fill it with ice and salt; let this briny water gravitate down through the roller and run into a tank below, then have a pump rigged up and pump the liquid back into the upper tank; thus you obtain cold water and use it over and over again, gaining more water all the time by the melting of the ice.   It will surprise you how fast the ice disappears when running this contrivance in summer.   Therefore, if you have time and receivers enough, it will pay you to keep your lard over night and run it the next morning.

Recipe No. 21

At what Temperature to Draw Lard
From the Agitator

RECIPE NO. 21
AT WHAT TEMPERATURE
TO DRAW LARD FROM THE
AGITATOR

Lard compound or choice family lard should not be drawn from the agitator until it has got to such a point that it is THICK. Then only should it be drawn into packages.

Recipe No. 22

Special Tables for Figuring Hardness
For Different Climates

91

RECIPE NO. 22
SPECIAL TABLES FOR
FIGURING HARDNESS FOR
DIFFERENT CLIMATES

Here are a number of tables that will enable you to figure up the hardness necessary for different climates, so that after reaching warm or cold countries the lard will be of a proper texture, thus securing its prompt sale.

In figuring this you must take into consideration first, the hardness of the ingredients to be used.

LARD-STEARINE is TWICE as hard as Lard

TALLOW is a GRADE HARDER than Lard

OLEO-STEARINE is THREE TIMES as hard as Lard

Cotton Oil and Lard take care of themselves.

Now, for instance, we prepare a formula of, say

40 per cent Lard
20 per cent Cotton Oil
20 per cent Tallow
20 per cent Oleo-stearine
100 per cent.

How does this compare in hardness with lard? For, of course, in figuring we take lard as the basis of hardness.

Now— 40 Lard = 40 Lard
    20 Oil = 20 Oil
              60 per cent

        20 Tallow . . . . . 1 time = 20
        20 Oleo-stearine. 3 times = 60
                          80 per cent

Now take   80 per cent
           Less 60 per cent
           Balance. 20 per cent . . . This shows that the product made according to this formula is 20 PER CENT HARDER THAN LARD.

Now take a formula of   75 per cent Oil
                        25 per cent Oleo-stearine
                     100 per cent.

The 75 per cent of oil stands; figure the hardness of the 25 per cent of oleo-stearine

        25 × 3 = 75 per cent Hardness
   now subtract from 75 per cent Oil
           the 75 per cent Extra-hardness
       Balance. 00 per cent. . . . . This shows that a formula of 75 per cent oil and 25 per cent oleo-stearine would make a product exactly equal to lard itself in hardness.

A formula of say   80 per cent Oil
                 5 per cent Oleo-stearine
              15 per cent Tallow
           100 per cent

would be figured as follows ·

5 × 3 Oleo-stearine 15 per cent	80 per cent Oil
15 Tallow. . . . . 15 per cent	deduct 30 per cent
30 per cent	Balance. 50 per cent

This shows the product from this formula to be 50 per cent softer than lard.

Compound lard should always be softer than prime steam lard in winter, and such a formula of 50 PER CENT SOFTER THAN LARD is all right for winter; in summer a formula of 30 PER CENT HARDER THAN LARD would be all right.

The best formulas for a lard that will not crumble can be easily figured out by following the above tables. A lard that is to be shipped to a warm climate should, of course, be HARDER THAN PRIME STEAM LARD and one that is destined for a cold climate, SOFTER THAN PRIME STEAM LARD. Be sure to always find out where the product is to be shipped before you manufacture it according to this or that formula.

Recipe No. 23

European Formulas

RECIPE NO. 23

EUROPEAN FORMULAS

The European lards are generally made from formulas composed of pure lard only.

Their summer formula is:

> 80 lbs. Prime Steam
> 20 lbs. Lard-stearine
> Total, 100 lbs.

In cooler weather less lard stearine is used.

There is also some demand for compound lard and this is made according to the price it is to be sold for. I might insert herein a number of formulas but, after all, the lards are to be made in accordance with the prices they sell for. Taking as a basis compound lard, choice family, etc., you just change the ingredients, either adding more of the higher-priced grade or reducing the quantity of the said grade and adding some of the lower-priced grade, such as tallow, cotton oil and deodorized greases. Of course this is easily figured out.

Recipe No. 24

Best Modes of Rendering Tallow
with Steam

RECIPE NO. 24
BEST MODES OF RENDERING
TALLOW WITH STEAM

Have a tank strong enough to stand a pressure of 90 lbs.
working pressure to the square inch; put into this tank your rough
fat and add a little water; then put on steam and cook for about
NINE hours with 60 or 70 lbs. pressure.   You will then produce a
fine tallow, dry and hard, and one that will bring a better price for
lard purposes than a low-cooked tallow, for it will have the flavor
of prime steam lard.   Being well cooked, the fibers will impregnate
the tallow with this desirable odor, especially when using it in compound lard.   On the opposite page will be found an engraving
of the most improved rendering tank.   This is made by the Murray
Iron Works Co., and is used in all the large packing houses,

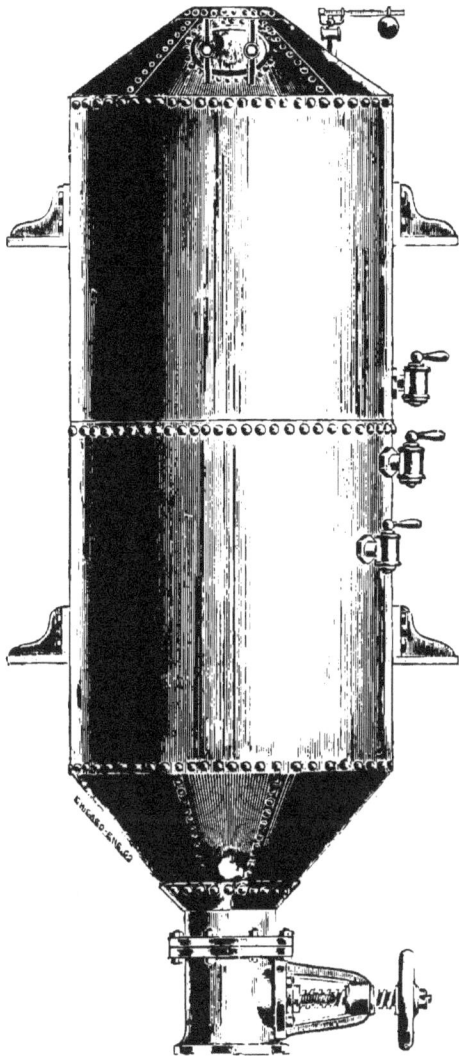

PACKERS'
RENDING
TANK

These tanks are
made of steel plate
throughout, a n d
can be had in any
size desired. They
are supplied with
quick opening gate
valves and fittings
as shown in the ac-
companying cut.

97

Recipe No. 25

How to Harden Tallow

RECIPE NO. 25
HOW TO HARDEN TALLOW

To harden tallow, use for every 100 lbs. tallow a mixture of

One-half lb. Sulphuric Acid
One-half lb. Nitric Acid.

Melt the tallow and stir continuously, then run the above mixture into it slowly; then allow to settle.   Draw off the acid water and wash well with clear water.
. This will make a white, odorless tallow; of course there will be quite a good deal of gas developed, which must be carried off through a large pipe or hood placed over the tank whenever the stock is being treated in this way.

Recipe No. 26

How to Bleach Tallow

103

RECIPE NO. 26

HOW TO BLEACH TALLOW

Take the tallow to be bleached and put it into the refining tank; melt it and heat it up to 220 degrees Fahrenheit. Add from 7 to 10 per cent of fuller's earth to the tallow, allowing the blower or air-pump to agitate the stock thoroughly. When the fuller's earth has been added, start the tallow through the filter; then cool and pack as desired

Machinery

Required for Making Oleomargarine

103

MACHINERY REQUIRED
FOR MAKING OLEOMARGARINE

This machinery is to include :

1ST. Wooden Tanks to put the fat in at the earliest moment after it has been taken from the animal; in these tanks the fat is washed and thoroughly chilled to eliminate all of the animal heat; from there it is taken to

2D. A Hasher.

3D. A Jacket Tank with an Agitator; then settled and al lowed to run into

4TH. Settling Tanks; then into

5TH. Coolers on Wheels.

6TH. Then into the seeding room and allowed to grain; then placed in cloths and put into

7TH. Presses. to be pressed.

An illustration of the most approved press for this purpose will be found on the following pages.

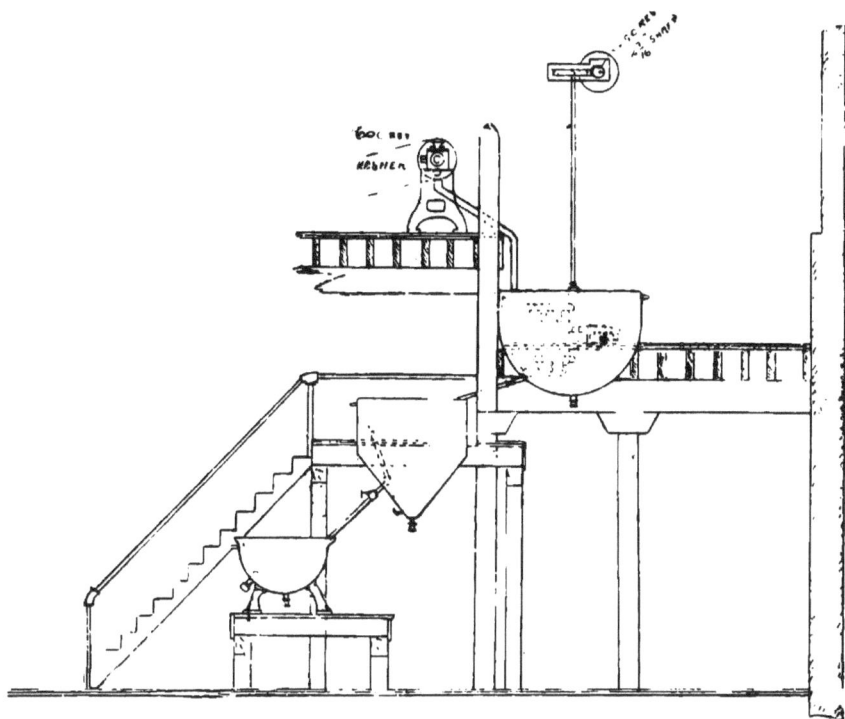

Side Elevation —

Figure 1

OLEOMARGARINE
DEPARTMENT

This engraving shows the hasher, jacket tank with agitator, and the settling tanks. This arrangement of machinery will be found most convenient when fitting up an oleomargarine plant.

107

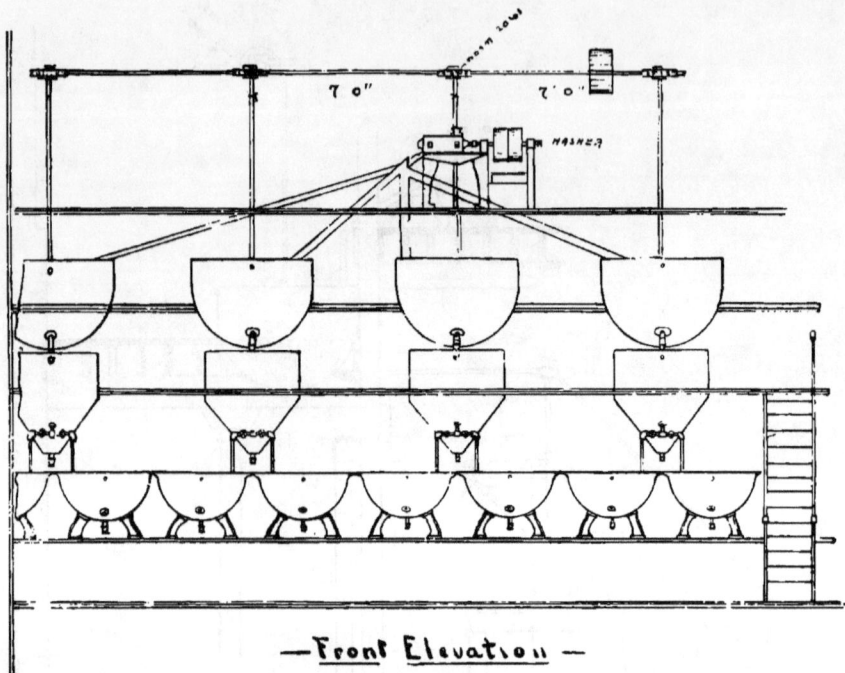

— Front Elevation —

Figure II

OLEOMARGARINE
DEPARTMENT

This engraving shows a front elevation of the oleomargarine plant,
the side elevation of which appears on the preceding page.

Recipe No. 27

Selection and Preparation of Fats
For Oleomargarine

RECIPE NO. 27
SELECTION AND PREPARATION
OF FATS
FOR OLEOMARGARINE

The selection and care of the fats are among the most important points in the manufacturing of oleomargarine, oleo-butter or butterine.

The best fats for making a No. 1 oil, such as is in great demand abroad, are obtained from the fat of cattle which is termed "long fat."   No mutton fat must be used.

The moment the animal is killed, the fat should be put into water and thoroughly washed, the animal heat being thus taken out.   Fat left lying about, even for two hours only, will not make a first-class oil.

Recipe No. 28

How to Manufacture Oleomargarine Oleo=Oil, Oleo=Butter and Butterine

111

RECIPE NO. 28
HOW TO MANUFACTURE
OLEOMARGARINE, OLEO-OIL
OLEO-BUTTER AND BUTTERINE

The first step after the fat has been cleaned, washed and thoroughly chilled, so that no animal heat remains, is to take it and cut it up into small pieces about the size of the hand.

It is then put in a hasher, so that all the fibers and tissues shall be torn asunder.

From this hasher it drops into an agitating jacket kettle, where it is heated to about 130 degrees Fahrenheit, NO MORE. It is then allowed to remain in this kettle until it is melted and settled.

In settling, use large quantities of coarse salt.

After it is settled, it is drawn off into settling jackets, where it is allowed to settle still more, being heated so as to stand at a temperature of about 120 degrees Fahrenheit.

After being again well settled, it is drawn off into coolers on wheels.

Never allow this stock to run DIRECT into the coolers, but run it through the finest hair-sieves you can obtain. The reason for this is that when melting fat at such a low temperature, there will always be found suspended small fibers or tissues; these, not being thoroughly cooked, are apt to get into the oil, and if they do get into it they will decompose and thus spoil a lot of stock. Be very careful on this point, as it is surprising what a very little it takes to spoil an otherwise excellent oil.

After the stock is run into these coolers on wheels it is wheeled into what is called the seeding room. The temperature in this room must be kept at from 75 to 80 degrees Fahrenheit. Never allow the thermometer in this room to vary much from these figures. Here the stock is allowed to remain from 24 to 30 hours, when it will be found to have granulated and look very much like granulated sugar; it will form a solid like mass with oil interspersed; the solid part is crystallized stearine. When the stock has this appearance it is ready for the press. It is then filled into cloths, set in molds, wrapped up and put into the press to be pressed by a gradually increasing pressure, under which the oil is extracted, leaving the oleo-stearine in the cloths. This press-room should have a temperature of about 89 to 92 degrees Fahrenheit

If the fat has been properly handled from the start, a clear, yellow, sweet oil is pressed and this oil is what is termed OLEO-MARGARINE-OIL or BUTTER-OIL.

Now, when oleo-butter is to be made, this oil is taken and cooled to about 70 degrees Fahrenheit.

About 100 lbs. of the oil, with about 15 to 20 lbs. of sour milk, are placed in a churn. Two and a half ounces of solution of Annetto, containing one-half to three-fourths of an ounce of solution of bicarbonate of soda, may then be added to the whole; then the mixture is agitated for about 15 to 20 minutes, when it is at once run into a tank on wheels, containing pounded ice, the mess running into the ice and being continually mixed with shovels or pitchforks until sufficiently cooled and chilled. Generally one man on each side of the tank is used to mix the stock well through the pounded ice.

By this process the grain is completely broken, and the butter will be as smooth as desired.

After remaining in contact with the ice for 2 or 3 hours, it is then dumped on an inclined table and crumbled up, so that all the ice will melt out.   Then about 30 lbs. at a time are put into a churn, with 20 to 25 lbs. of sour milk, and the whole is churned for about 15 minutes.

By this last process the flavor and odor desired are imparted to the butter; then the working, draining and salting (three-fourths of an ounce of salt to the pound), complete the manufacturing.

European Processes

For Manufacturing Oleomargarine, Etc.

EUROPEAN PROCESSES
FOR MANUFACTURING OLEO-
MARGARINE, ETC.

An account of the most recent European processes for manufacturing oleomargarine, etc., is here in order.

Those processes consist :

1ST. In washing the fat.
2D. In crystallizing the fat.
3D. In pressing the crystallized fat.
4TH. In churning with cotton oil, etc., and milk

The fresh suet is first freed from all adhering tissues and is then thrown into large tubs, wherein the blood is carefully washed off by means of cold water.

It is then put through a meat hasher, where it is cut and drawn up into a white mass, which is delivered into a kettle jacketed with warm water and supplied with a stirring apparatus. Here it is warmed up to 122 degrees Fahrenheit with constant agitation for two hours.

The stirring is then stopped, water is introduced and the rendered fat is forced through a pipe into the jacketed tub. From there it is drawn into small trays, and in 24 hours it is cooled down to 80 degrees Fahrenheit, when it is wrapped in cloths and put in a hydraulic press, as shown on page 118, and the oleomargarine (a mixture of stearine, palmatine and oleoine) is squeezed out of it.

The oleomargarine oil is then put into a churn, together with milk, cotton oil and a little butter color.   In fifteen minutes the churning is completed.   The churned mass is then worked in the same manner as butter, to remove the milk and water.

Artificial butter, thus carefully prepared. will keep for months without becoming rancid.

HEAVY HYDRAULIC
LARD AND TALLOW PRESS

This illustration shows a very heavy hydraulic press for large manufacturers or for those who buy and re-press cracklins. The hoop is 30 inches in diameter by 40 inches in depth, composed of heavy steel bands and staves of sufficient strength to sustain the great pressure. The plunger is so attached to the head of the press that it can be swung to one side, uncovering a part of the hoop for filling. The face of the plunger is heated by steam. The platen or saucer on which the hoop rests is also steam heated, the connections for steam being telescoped so as to allow for the rise and fall. Thus the cracklin is pressed between hot plates and a larger percentage of grease can be extracted. In operating, when the cracklin is sufficiently pressed and the hoop is at its highest point, the dogs on center rods are turned under one of the bands. The platen then being run down leaves the hoop suspended. Blocks now being set underneath the lower band and press run up again, the cracklin is forced out of the hoops and drops on the saucer, from whence it can be removed. The blocks are then removed and press run up until the hoop rests on the platen, the dogs on rods are thrown out and hoop again lowered. It is more easily and quickly operated than where the hoop is made to open. Power, 500 tons; weight, 2,800 lbs. This press is made by the Boomer & Boschert Press Co.

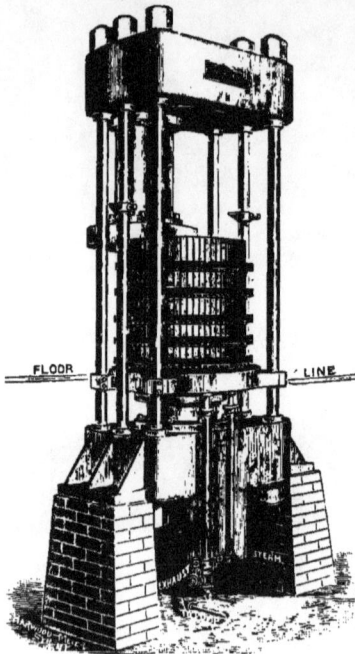

Chemical Comparison

Between Oleo=Butter and Natural Butter

119

CHEMICAL COMPARISON
BETWEEN OLEO-BUTTER AND
NATURAL BUTTER

A natural butter contains:

	FAT	CASEINE	ASH	WATER
Good quality .	86.06	0.42	0.12	13.77
Poor to bad	82.60	0.72	0.20	17.08
Fresh Hay Butter . . .	70.19	2.59	0.25	26.19
Common Cow Butter .	86.06	0.40	0.14	13.77

An oleo-butter contains:

	FAT	CASEINE	ASH	WATER
Oleomargarine-butter .	86.24	1.20	. . .	12.56
Other brands of Oleo .	87.15	0.57	1.63	15.50

Recipe No. 29

To prepare the Leaf for Making
Neutral

RECIPE NO. 29
TO PREPARE THE LEAF FOR
MAKING NEUTRAL

Take the leaf lard and hang it in a cold place; allow it to hang for 24 hours, so that all the animal heat is taken out. In hanging great care must be taken not to allow the leaf to overlap, as it will prevent the animal heat from leaving it. The pieces must be hung up smooth and not allowed to touch one another.

Recipe No. 30

How to Manufacture Wet and
Dry Neutral

RECIPE NO. 30

HOW TO MANUFACTURE WET
AND DRY NEUTRAL

The leaf, after being thoroughly cooled, so that no more animal heat remains in it, is taken and hashed at a low temperature,
not over 160 degrees Fahrenheit.   There it is treated in about
the same manner as when manufacturing oleo.   It is then allowed
to settle and is run into another jacket tank.   It now being freed
from all fibers and tissues, it is heated to 200 degrees Fahrenheit.
From this jacket it is run into small tanks of strong brine holding
about 500 pounds.

It is allowed to remain in this water for twelve hours.   A
small percentage of nitric acid has been added to this water to
deodorize the lard.   The next day the plug is pulled out and the
water let off; then fresh water is added and the stock well stirred
and washed, so as to wash out of it all the acid water.   It is generally allowed to remain in fresh water over night, always keeping
the water COLD.

WET NEUTRAL is drained and packed, and sold with a certain amount "off" for the water.

DRY NEUTRAL.—To manufacture same, the wet neutral
stock is placed in a jacket and very slowly heated, not over 110
degrees Fahrenheit.   Then it is allowed to settle, the water is
drawn off, and the stock is drawn into tierces for shipment.

Always draw the neutral, to ship it, when it is as COLD as
possible; never do so when it is hot or warm; be sure that it is
COLD.

Laws of the Different States

Governing the Manufacture and Sale
of Oleomargarine

123

LAWS OF THE DIFFERENT STATES GOVERNING THE MANUFACTURE AND SALE OF OLEOMARGARINE

ALABAMA.—This State has no laws on the subject.

ARKANSAS.—This State has no laws on the subject.

CALIFORNIA.—"An act to prevent the sale of oleomargarine under the name and pretense that the said commodity is butter." This law is restrictive, requiring the word "oleomargarine" to be branded on the package. The penalty is a fine of from $50 to $200, or imprisonment from 50 to 200 days, or both.

"An act to prevent fraud and deception in the sale of butter and cheese." This law is restrictive, requiring the article to be manufactured and sold under its appropriate name. The penalty is a fine of from $10 to $500, or imprisonment 10 to 90 days, or both. Approved March 2, 1891.

"An act to prevent the sale or disposition as butter of the substance known as 'oleomargarine' or 'oleomargarine butter,' and, when oleomargarine or oleomargarine butter is sold or disposed of, requiring notice thereof to be given." This law is restrictive, requiring branding of packages, and also requiring hotel-keepers, etc., to keep posted up in their places of business, in three places, the words "Oleomargarine is sold here." The penalty is a fine of from $5 to $500 or imprisonment for not more than three months, or both. Approved March 1, 1883.

"An act to protect and encourage the production of pure and wholesome milk, and to prohibit and punish the production and sale of unwholesome or adulterated milk." This law makes it a misdemeanor to sell or expose for sale adulterated or unwholesome milk, or to keep cows, for producing the same, in an unhealthy condition, or to feed them on feed that will produce impure milk, etc. The penalty is a fine of from $1 to $100 for the first offense, and double that amount for each subsequent offense. Approved March 12, 1870.

COLORADO.—"An act to encourage the sale of milk and to provide penalties for the adulteration thereof." This law makes it a misdemeanor to sell adulterated milk or milk from which the cream has been taken off, or to withdraw the strippings without the purchasers being made aware of the fact. The penalty is from $25 to $100, or imprisonment for not more than six months, or both. Approved May 20, 1881.

"An act to regulate the manufacture and sale of oleomargarine, butterine or other substances made in imitation of or having the semblance of butter, and to provide penalties for the violation of the provisions thereof." This law requires that a license be obtained before manufacturing, importing or selling oleomargarine or kindred products within the State. The cost of the license to manufacture to be not less than $1,000; that of the license to sell not less than $500. The penalties to be a fine of from $50 to $500, or imprisonment not to exceed one year, or both. Approved April 6, 1885.

CONNECTICUT.—"An act concerning the sale of oleomargarine and other articles." This law requires that the article shall be properly branded, and that the seller shall keep a sign posted up in his place of business that such commodity is sold here. The penalty is a fine of $7, or imprisonment from 10 to 30 days, or both. Approved April 4, 1883.

DELAWARE.—"An act to regulate the sale of oleomargarine." This law is restrictive in its nature. Penalty, a $50 fine; commitment until the fine is paid. Approved February 10, 1879.

"An act to annul Chapter 154, Vol. 16, of the Laws of Delaware." This amendment has reference to the fact that the substance manufactured is artificial butter.

FLORIDA.—Chapter 80, sections 34 and 35 of McLellan's Digest, 1881. Section 34 makes it a misdemeanor to sell spurious preparations as butter. Section 35 has reference to hotels and boarding houses. Penalties not to exceed a fine of $100. or imprisonment for 30 days, or both.

GEORGIA.—This State has no law on the subject.

ILLINOIS.—"An act to prevent and punish the adulteration of food, drink and medicine, and the sale thereof when adulterated." Section 3 of this law has reference to coloring matter in food, drink or medicine. Section 4 of this law refers to the mixing of oleomargarine with butter, cheese, etc., and it requires the seller to inform the buyer of the fact and of the preparations of the mixture. The penalties are: First offense, a $25 to $200 fine; second offense, a $100 to $200 fine and imprisonment from 1 to 6 months, or both; third offense, a fine of from $500 to $2,000 and imprisonment not less than 1 year nor more than 5 years, or both. Approved June 1, 1881.

"An act requiring operators of butter and cheese factories on the corporation plan to give bonds, and prescribing penalties for the violation thereof." This law requires the filing of a bond, in the penal sum of $6,000, that certain reports will be made on the first of each month, and a copy filed with the town clerk, etc. The penalties are a fine of from $200 to $500, or imprisonment from 30 days to 6 months, or both. Approved June 18, 1883.

INDIANA.—Section 2071 of the Revised Statutes refers to the selling of unwholesome milk. This section provides against the sale of unwholesome milk, rendered such either by adulteration or by the feed given the cows; also against the use of poisonous or deleterious matters in the manufacturing of butter and cheese. The penalty is a fine of from $50 to $500.

"An act to prevent the sale of impure butter and the keeping on any table in any hotel or boarding house of impure butter, and to provide penalties." This law requires the branding of the packages with the word "Oleomargarine." Penalty, a fine of from $10 to $50. Approved March 3, 1883.

IOWA.—Section 4042 of the Code. This section provides against the adulteration of milk in any way. Penalty, a $25 to $100 fine. It makes also the offender liable in double that amount to the party injured.

"An act to protect the dairy interest and for the punishment of fraud connected therewith." This law requires that packages containing oleomargarine and kindred products shall be branded with the word "Oleomargarine," and provides penalties of from $20 to $100 fine, or imprisonment from 10 to 90 days, or both.

"An act to prevent and punish the adulteration of articles

of food, drink and medicine, and the sale thereof when adulterated." This law provides that skimmed-milk cheese shall be so branded; and when oleomargarine is mixed with any other substance for sale, that it shall be distinctly branded with the true and appropriate name. Penalties: First offense, from $10 to $50 fine; second offense, from $25 to $100 fine, or to be confined in the county jail not more than 30 days; third offense, fine $500 to $1,000, or imprisonment for not less than 1 year and not more than 5 years, or both.

KANSAS has no law on the subject.

KENTUCKY has no law on the subject.

LOUISIANA has no law on the subject.

MARYLAND.—"An act to repeal the Act of 1883, Chapter 493 entitled 'An act for the protection of the dairymen, and to prevent deception in the sale of butter and cheese,' and to re-enact new sections in lieu thereof." This law requires that substances made in semblance of butter and cheese, not being the true products of the dairy, shall be branded with the word "Oleomargarine," making same conspicuous, so that the buyer shall be apprised of the nature of the article he has bought. Penalties: A fine of $100 for the first offense; for the second offense, an imprisonment of not less than 30 days and not more than 90 days; for the third offense, an imprisonment of not less than 3 months or more than one year. Approved April 8, 1884.

MAINE.—"An act to amend Chapter 128 of the Revised Statutes relating to the sale of unwholesome food." This law is prohibitory as to oleomargarine and kindred products, the penalties being, for the first offense, a fine of $100, and for each subsequent offense, a fine of $200, to be recovered with costs.

MASSACHUSETTS.—This State has a law against the sale of adulterated milk. Penalty for the first offense: a $50 to $100 fine; for the second offense, a fine of $100 to $300, or imprisonment from 30 to 60 days; for subsequent offenses, a $50 fine, and imprisonment from 60 to 90 days

MICHIGAN.—"An act to prevent deception in the manufacture and sale of dairy products, and to preserve public health." This law prohibits the manufacture and sale of oleomargarine and kindred products. The penalty provided for the first offense is a fine of not less than $200 and not more than $500, or imprisonment of not less than 6 months and not more than 1 year, or both; for each subsequent offense, imprisonment for 1 year. Approved June 12, 1885.

MINNESOTA.—"An act to prevent the sale and manufacture of unhealthy or adulterated dairy products." This law prohibits the sale of impure or adulterated milk. Penalties: For the first offense, a fine of from $25 to $50, or an imprisonment of from 1 to 6 months, or both; for each subsequent offense, 6 months' imprisonment. This law also prohibits the manufacture and sale of oleaginous substances or compounds of the same. Penalties for the first offense: a fine of from $100 to $500, or imprisonment from 6 months to 1 year, or both; for each subsequent offense, a 1 year imprisonment. Approved March 6, 1885.

MISSISSIPPI. —This State has no laws on the subject.

MISSOURI.—This State adopted the first prohibitory law concerning the matter. The penalty provided is a fine not to exceed $1,000, or confinement in the county jail not to exceed one year, or both.

NEBRASKA.— Section 2345 of the State statutes refers to skimmed and adulterated milk. This section provides against the sale of such adulterated milk, and fixes the penalty to be a $25 to $100 fine, the delinquent to be, besides, liable in double the amount of his fine toward the person or persons upon whom the fraud has been perpetrated.

NEVADA.—This State has no law on the subject.

NEW HAMPSHIRE.—"An act relating to imitation butter." This law provides that no artificial butter shall be sold unless it is colored PINK. The penalty for the first offense is a fine of $50, and for the second offense, a fine of $100. A certificate of the analysis, sworn to by the analyzer, shall be admitted in evidence in all prosecutions; the expense of said analysis, not exceeding $20, to be included in the costs.

NEW JERSEY and NEW YORK.— In these two States the law in reference to oleomargarine is practically prohibitory

NORTH CAROLINA.—The State has no law on the subject.

OHIO.—This State has a law which is prohibitory except concerning oleomargarine made out of beef-suet and milk. The penalty for the first offense is a fine of from $100 to $500, or a 3 to 6 month imprisonment, or both, and for all subsequent offenses, the same fine and imprisonment up to one year. Approved April 27, 1885.

OREGON.—The law in this state provides against adulterated and unwholesome milk, against keeping cows in an unhealthy condition, and against feeding them upon unhealthy feed. It also provides that oleaginous substances sold upon the market shall be so branded as to distinguish them from the true dairy products, and that in hotels, boarding houses, restaurants, etc., where such substances are used as articles of food, the bill of fare shall state the fact, and that the name of such substance shall be posted up in the dining-room in a conspicuous place.   Approved February 20, 1885.

PENNSYLVANIA.—"An act to protect dairymen and to prevent deception in sales of butter and cheese."   This act requires the branding of imitation butter and cheese   The penalty is a fine of $100 for importation of the products in violation of this act; otherwise the penalty is a fine of from $5 to $200, or imprisonment of from 10 to 30 days, or both.   Approved May 24, 1883.

"An act for the protection of public health, and to prevent adulteration of dairy products and fraud in the sales thereof." This law prohibits the sale of oleomargarine and kindred products.   Penalties: For the first offense, a fine of from $100 to $300, or imprisonment from 10 to 30 days; for each subsequent offense, imprisonment for one year.   Approved May 1, 1885.

RHODE ISLAND.   "An act concerning the sale of butter, potatoes, onions, berries, nuts and shell-beans."   This law provides that imitation butter shall be stamped "Oleomargarine," and that the retailer shall deliver to the purchaser a label upon which shall be the word "Oleomargarine."   The penalty is a $1 fine.

SOUTH CAROLINA.—There is no law in this State relating to the subject.

TENNESSEE.— The code of 1884. Chapter 14, Sections 2682,

2683, 2684, treats of the subject. This law requires that the substance be manufactured and sold under its true and appropriate name, and be distinctly branded with the said true and appropriate name. The penalty is a fine of from $10 to $300 or imprisonment of from 10 to 90 days.

TEXAS.—This state has no law on the subject.

VERMONT.—"An act to prevent fraud in the sale of oleomargarine and other substances as butter." This law provides that oleomargarine and kindred products shall not be sold as butter. Penalty, a $500 fine. Approved November, 1884.

Chapter 192, laws 1874,76 of 1870 and 51 of 1855, provided against the adulteration of milk.

VIRGINIA.—The Code of Virginia of 1873, Chapter 865, Title 26, Section 56, provides against adulterating milk intended for the manufacture of cheese; it provides against the adulteration of milk carried to cheese factories, etc. The penalty is a fine of from $25 to $100, with costs of suits.

WEST VIRGINIA.—Chapter 41, Acts of W. Virginia, 1885. "An act to prevent the manufacture and sale of mixed and impure butter and cheese and imitation thereof." This law requires that the true and appropriate name of the substance shall be printed thereon, etc. Penalty, a $10 to $100 fine.

WISCONSIN.—Section 1496, Chapter 61 of the Revised Statutes of Wisconsin. This act provides that no cream shall be taken from the manufacturing where the milk is to be worked up: also that the person manufacturing cheese at factories shall keep certain records.

Chapter 361, Revised Statutes. "An act to prevent the manufacture and sale of oleaginous substances or compounds of the same in imitation of the pure dairy products, and to repeal Section 143 of Chapter 49 of the laws of 1881." This law prohibits the manufacture and sale of oleomargarine and kindred products. The penalty not to exceed a fine of $1,000 or imprisonment for one year, or both. Approved April 13, 1885.

ALASKA.—Has no laws on the subject.

ARIZONA. "An act to regulate the manufacture and sale of oleomargarine and other substances in the territory of Arizona." This law requires that oleomargarine and kindred substances sold in the territory shall be appropriately branded with the word "Oleomargarine," and that the seller shall deliver to the buyer a printed label on which is the word "Oleomargarine." Also that dealers shall keep posted up in their place of business this sign: "Oleomargarine sold here." Penalties: First offense, a fine of not less than $5; for the second offense, a fine of not less than $100 or imprisonment for 60 days, and each subsequent offense, a fine of $500 and imprisonment for 90 days. Approved March 8, 1883.

DAKOTA.- [Law approved when it was still a territory, and now in force in the States of NORTH DAKOTA and SOUTH DAKOTA.] "An act to secure the public health and safety against unwholesome provisions." This law requires that all oleaginous substances shall be branded with their true and proper names. Cost of analysis, not to exceed $20, can or may be included in the cost of prosecutions. Penalties: For the first offense, $100, and for every other offense. $200 Bill passed at the session of 1883.

IDAHO has no laws on the subject.

MONTANA has no laws on the subject.

NEW MEXICO has no laws on the subject.

UTAH has no laws on the subject.

WASHINGTON has no laws on the subject.

Recipes Nos. 31
32 and 33

Latest and Most Approved Modes of Caring
for Blood, Bones and Offal

RECIPES NOS. 31, 32 AND 33
LATEST AND MOST APPROVED MODES
OF CARING FOR
BONES, BLOOD AND OFFAL

No. 31.   THE BONES are dried and sold for different purposes.
The jaw-bones and skulls are sold to sugar refiners, who use them for filtering molasses and syrups; they grind them and burn them.

The shin-bones are put in cold water over night, the water soaking in and causing the marrow to leave the bones.   They are then washed in warm water and a little sal soda is added to whiten the bones.   Never boil the water; just warm it enough so that it will not scald your hand.   After the bones are in the water a few hours, they are cleaned and put away to dry.   These bones are used for making brush-handles, knife-handles, etc., and are always in demand at a good price.

No. 32.   BLOOD is caught in a tank, where open steam is put into it and it is allowed to cook until it thickens, stirring it occasionally until it coagulates.   It is then taken out, put into bags and pressed.   Then it is put into the drier and left there until it is thoroughly dried, when it is removed and spread on the floor until all the heat is out.   Finally, it is packed into sacks and stored or shipped ready for market.

No. 33. THE OFFAL is tanked and cooked for six hours; it is then treated the same as the blood, pressed and dried. This product, after being dried, is termed "Tankage Fertilizer." The dried blood is termed "Blood Tankage," and is worth considerably more than the former for making fertilizer. Both are analyzed before being bought, and are sold at so much per unit of ammonia. Both blood and offal should be worked up as soon as possible, so as not to allow either to decompose, as, by decomposing, they deteriorate in value and lose their strength of ammonia.

Recipe No. 34

How Glycerine is Obtained and Manufac=
tured into a Chemically
Pure Article

141

RECIPE NO. 34

HOW GLYCERINE IS OBTAINED AND
MANUFACTURED INTO A
CHEMICALLY PURE ARTICLE

In the first place, the principle followed is that law in chemistry according to which a strong base, under favorable conditions,
will separate a weaker one from its acids, combining with the
acids and taking the place of the weaker base.   The fat is thus
saponified, a soap being formed which is decomposed next, the
fatty acids liberated and then separated.   In the last process begins the employment of mechanical instead of chemical means;
for, though repeated dilutions would effect a more perfect separation of the acids, the plan pursued is quicker, cheaper and suffi
ciently effective for the purpose desired.

The saponification of the fat is accomplished in an apparatus
called the "digester," an engraving of which will be found on the
opposite page.   It consists of a COPPER CYLINDER made of three-
fourths copper, about 20 ft. long and 3 ft. in diameter; a PUMP
arranged to force the contents from the bottom to the top of this
cylinder, into which the tallow has been run and mixed with one
and one-half to two per cent of slacked lime.

Say you use 5,000 lbs. of tallow, 2 per cent of lime would
be 100 lbs.; this is slacked and then the limewater is run into
this digester, the pump being started so as to keep the tallow
agitated while the limewater is running into it.   After the limewater is in, the pump is kept in motion until the operation is finished.   The digester is then closed and the steam allowed to

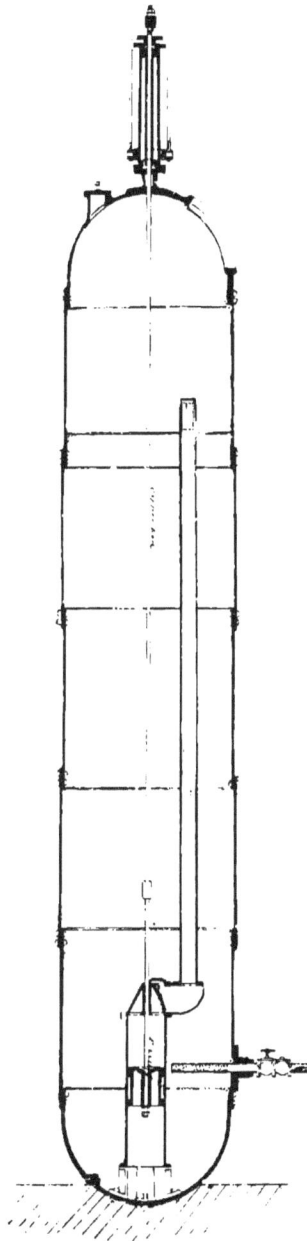

enter.   The mixture is heated to about 600 Fahrenheit by super-heated steam, which is let into the digester at a pressure of 250 lbs. per square inch.

The water, being the heavier, sinks to the bottom of the cop-per cylinder, whence it is pumped and thrown on a perforated plate above the fat, that it may fall through it in many little streams.

This operation is kept up for seven or eight hours, after which it is found that the lime has united with the fat acids and formed a lime-soap, whilst the water has consorted with the dissociated glycerine.

The contents of the digester are allowed to settle for one or two hours, when they will be found to be in two stratas, the lime-soap on top and the crude glycerine at the bottom.   These are then blown into two separate tanks by the power of steam.

It is from the candle manufacture that comes the enormous supply of glycerine which is now a very important article of com-merce.   A few years ago it was wasted; now it leaves the digester in a crude state and is put in a vacuum pan; the water is expelled and a thick syrup, of a dark color, left behind.   This is put through bone charcoal, filtered, distilled and ready for market. It is put to a great variety of uses, many of which depend upon its peculiar properties of non-volatility and absorption of atmos-pheric moisture.

Harness-makers and leather manufacturers use it in making leather pliable.

It is put into gas-meters because it does not freeze except at very low temperature.   Molders keep their clay moist with it. Tobacconists sweeten chewing tobacco with it and ladies apply it to their hands and faces to soften the skin.

In pharmacy, solutions or compounds of glycerine are more

M·J·FITCH
PAPER CO.

✳ ✳ ✳

RANDOLPH AND FRANKLIN STREETS,

CHICAGO, U.S.A.

CABLE ADDRESS:
"Dolphin, Chicago."

Manufacturers' Agents,

Importers and Jobbers of

Vegetable Parchment Papers

High Grade Ham Papers

Waxed Papers and

Packers' Papers

A Scrap of Paper.

DID YOU EVER stop to consider what it represents, the part it plays in the industrial economy of nations and the affairs of men — of what and how it is made, the relation it bears to YOUR business, and the many purposes for which it can be advantageously used by you? If not, drop us a line — drop us a line anyway. Ask questions of us and see what we will have to say.

We believe in the old adage, that "**TWO HEADS** are better than one." One head says what it wants; the other gets it. You want paper for wrapping meats, lining and covering lard packages and for many other purposes. We can get it for you. Any sort that is used in your own especial line of business; or, better still, if you have ideas of your own upon the subject, or wish to get a paper for some specific purpose, we can make it for you according to those ideas or to suit that purpose. In other words, our experience as PAPER MAKERS is at your command — if you want it.

VEGETABLE PARCHMENT PAPERS. FOR WRAPPING Smoked Hams and Bacon, Pork Loins and other Fresh Meats, Sausages, Dried Beef and Tongues.

An incomparable paper for the purpose; air-tight, water, grease and oil proof; lessens the percentage of shrinkage, prevents mold, and will not stick to the meat. Write for our circular and full sized sample sheets of the paper, stating the purpose for which it is to be used.

WAXED MANILA PAPERS. FOR WRAPPING PORK LOINS and other fresh meats and lining shipping boxes.

8 ¾ sheets to the pound. 24 x 36.

Guaranteed uniform quality and free from **TASTE** or **SMELL**.

ODD SIZES TO ORDER.

GLAZED DRAB HAM PAPERS. OUR No. 1 SILK FINISHED. ∴ ∴ ∴ ∴ Introduced by us in 1890.

Exclusively **OUR OWN SPECIALTY** and the standard canvasing paper now in use by the packing trade; **CLEAN, STRONG, PLIABLE** and **LEATHERY**; will not cut the hands, without odor, and guaranteed free from **SULPHUROUS ACID** and **GROUND WOOD.**

PARCHMENT CIRCLE TOPS. FOR COVERING BUTTERINE, Lard and Cotton Seed Oil Products.

Cut from white or blue parchment, and furnished, printed or plain. in all diameters, from one-half to twenty-two inches.

PARCHMENT PAIL LININGS. Cut from white or blue parchment, to fit lard tubs and pails.

They prevent Lard from absorbing the woody odor and flavor of the package, keeping it also from working through the seams of the package in warm weather.

Packages lined with them can be readily emptied of their entire contents by being turned upside down.

OUR FACILITIES ·· FOR ··· THE PRINTING OF PARCHMENT PAPER And for turning out work of a high grade and artistic merit are not to be excelled by anyone in the business. In this, as in all other departments, our motto is

" Not How Much, but How Good."

Our new process Silver Printing for white and blue lard tops will interest you. It is brighter and cleaner than silver bronze, and absolutely untarnishable.

stable than aqueous, oleaginous or saccharine preparations, while they are less stimulant and generally more agreeable than alcoholic tinctures. Glycerine is used advantageously in ointments to replace lard; it is mixed with pills to prevent their drying and becoming hard. For liniments it has no equal. A most excellent liniment is made by adding one part of carbolic acid to five of glycerine. It is a sovereign remedy for cuts, sores, ulcers, gangrenous wounds, etc. Every packing house should have a mixture of this liniment for man and beast, and it is highly recommended for horses galled by harness.

Glycerine, being altogether of an oily nature, is not prone to fermentation or decomposition; it does not become sour, rancid or gummy; it remains fluid even at a temperature where quicklime becomes frozen solid, and does not evaporate below 200 degrees Fahrenheit. For these reasons, it is most useful for the oiling of delicate and exposed machinery, such as tower-clocks, chronometers, surveying instruments, etc.

The question has often been asked me: "Is glycerine explosive?" To which I can answer: No; it is quite different from nitroglycerine, and possesses as much explosive power as olive oil. Nor is there a particle of danger in handling it. Nitroglycerine, however, is an explosive of wonderful power, very many times stronger than the best gunpowder.

Nitroglycerine is made by adding nitric acid and sulphuric acid to chemically pure glycerine. There are a great many glycerines upon the market sold as chemically pure and which look perfect, although a proper test will quickly prove that they are NOT chemically pure. I will give here one of the best and most practical tests, both simple and efficient, that will allow any one to detect the impurities that may occur in glycerine.

This test, called the "nitrate of silver test," is considered
Packers' En. 10

the most thorough and efficient of all by the leading glycerine manufacturers and by the United States Dispensary experts.

To make this test: Pour into a small white glass bottle four tablespoonfuls of glycerine and one-half teaspoonful of nitrate of silver solution; shake the mixture well and let it stand. If the glycerine be chemically pure the above mixture may assume a slight gray or red tinge after the lapse of several hours, owing to the partial decomposition of the nitrate of silver by the action upon it of the glycerine, but not the least sediment or deposit will be precipitated, even several days after the test has been made. Nor will the mixture when well shaken, at the latter time, become opaque or of a dark brown or black color; but it will remain transparent, whereas, if the glycerine be impure—containing fatty acids or other organic matter which will decompose and develop a marked odor in the course of time, or containing lime, chlorides, lead or sulphates—then the above mixture, after several hours, will become of a dark brown or black color, or it may show a heavy white or yellow precipitate, and if the mixture stands several days and is then well shaken, it will become a dark brown or black, opaque liquid.

The preparation for the above test is made by dissolving one part, by weight, of nitrate of silver crystal, which can be obtained at any drug store, in four parts of distilled water, and keeping the said solution from the light in a glass-stopped bottle.

Glucose or grape sugar is used to adulterate glycerine, and may be detected by heating the glycerine in a glass test-tube with a piece of caustic potash, when the sugar will be turned to a blackish color; if cane sugar be present it acquires a deep blue tint. The polariscope will also detect the presence of saccharine matter by polarizing transmitted light. whereas glycerine does not.

A prime quality of glycerine should have a gravity of 29½ degrees Beaume, at the standard temperature of 60 degrees Fahrenheit (the Beaume hydrometer used should have an enlarged scale, say of 1½ inch to the degree, each degree being divided into tenths), and the glycerine should be odorless and remain limpid when heated with a solution of nitrate of silver.

Not less than 3,200,000 lbs of glycerine are produced by the candle manufacturers of the United States and utilized every year in this country, and yet, as late as 1854, glycerine was considered worthless and allowed to run into the sewers. In that year the French candle manufacturers first began to manufacture candles by the new process, and, for a long time after, they permitted the lime-soap to become hard, and then ground it up to dissociate the lime from the fat acids. Now this is done without such delay; the liquid soap is run into lead-lined vats with a proportion of acid added; the chemical principle involved is the more laborious process of saponification; the glycerine base has been supplanted by the lime base, and this must now be got rid of. The sulphuric acid takes hold of the lime, forming a sulphate of lime, and acids float off free. On the following four pages will be found illustrations of a glycerine plant.

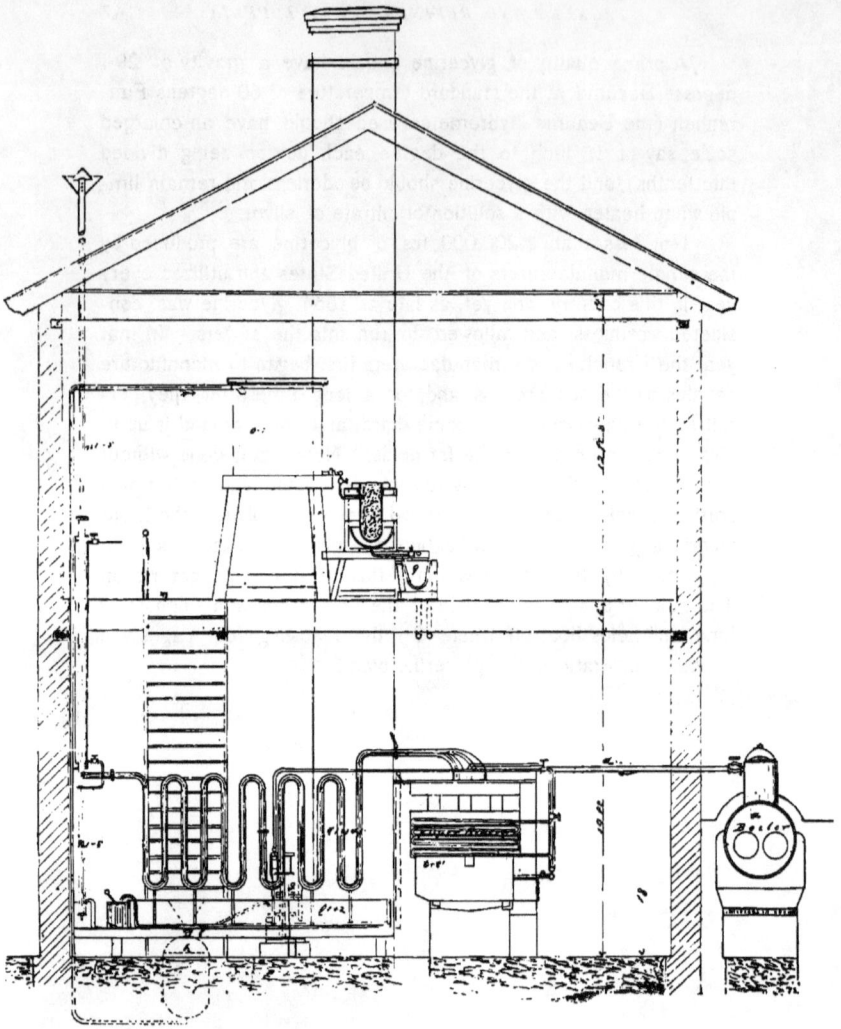

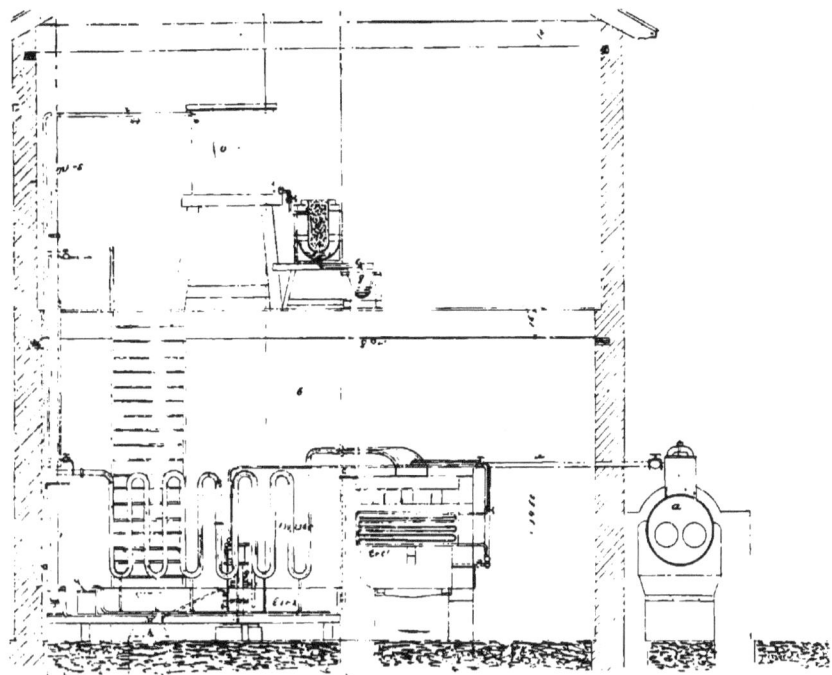

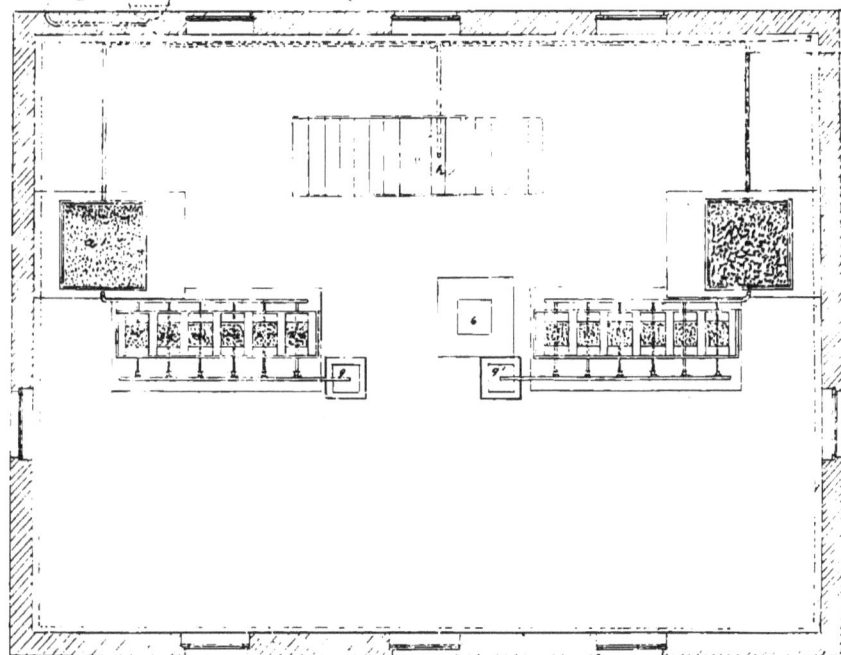

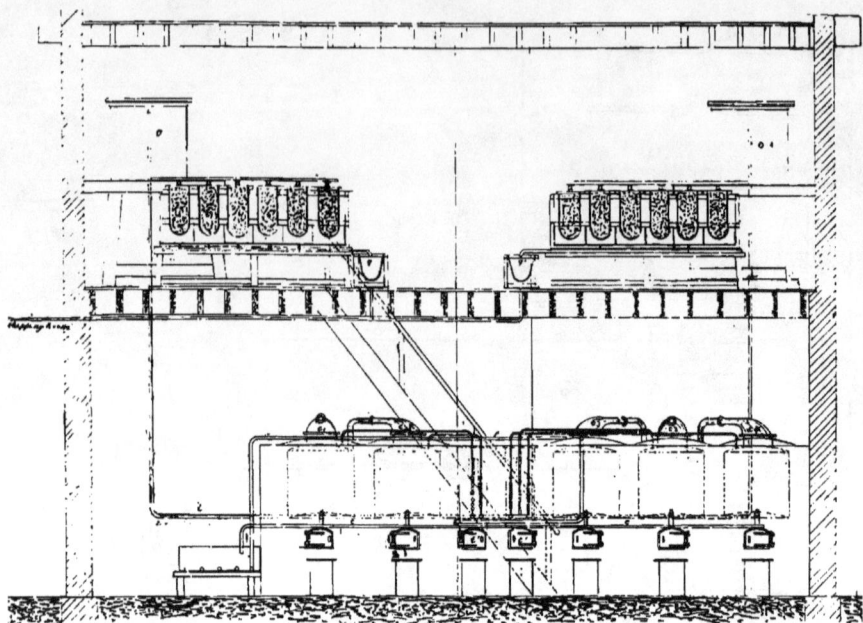

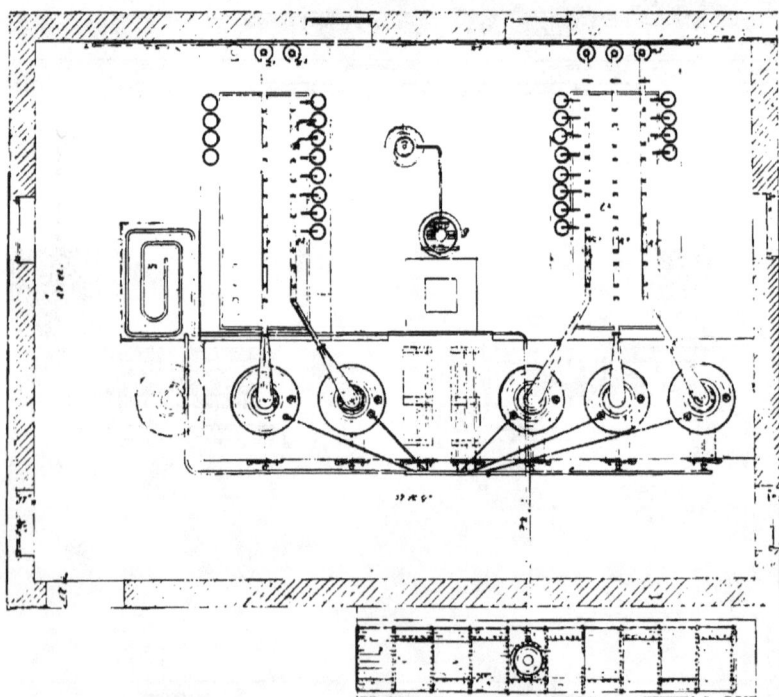

Glycerin Department.

Recipe No. 35

Purification and Bleaching
Of Fatty Acids

RECIPE NO. 35
PURIFICATION AND BLEACHING
OF FATTY ACIDS

Sulphuric acid is used for this process; for example:

Three quarters to one and a half per cent of the oil of vitriol will precipitate the mucilage and other matters; first it removes the water by which these substances were held in solution by the oil, and afterward clears the mucous matters themselves and renders them insoluble by effecting their destruction. A lead-lined tank is used, and also an open steam coil. The stock should be cooked about one hour and then allowed to settle.

Best Grade

Of Cotton Seed Oil

BEST GRADE OF
COTTON SEED OIL

The best grade of cotton seed oil to be used is that which has a light color, is free from any odor, and is called "Butter Oil."

Refined cotton oil has a specific gravity of 0.9264 at 59 degrees Fahrenheit.

Best Brand

Of Fuller's Earth and Where
it Comes From

157

BEST BRAND OF FULLER'S
EARTH AND WHERE IT
COMES FROM

I have found that the fuller's earth furnished by the Hickey & Spieker Company, Chicago, Ill., has given me the best results. It seems that the mine they work produces the strongest fuller's earth.

Recipe No. 36

How to Adulterate Oils

RECIPE NO. 36

HOW TO ADULTERATE OILS

Use neutral oil. This is used by nearly all compounders and mixers of oil. A good neutral oil will stand a cold test of between 20 and 30 degrees above zero, Fahrenheit; there are, of course, different grades. The light colored oil is from 33 to 34 specific gravity; the dark oil from 31 to 32. There is no fixed rule regarding the use of these oils for mixing with animal oils. Some use 5 gallons to a barrel of animal oil, such as lard oil; some use 10 gallons, and I have used, myself, as much as 15 gallons to the barrel, and I have known as much as 20 gallons to be used, or, in other words, 30 gallons of lard oil and 20 gallons of neutral oil. I consider 20 per cent a good mixture; and I think a lard oil, for some purposes, mixed to this extent is even better than in its pure state, as the neutral oil will have a tendency to prevent corrosion of metal, while, of course, it cheapens the cost of lard oil.

The dark neutral oil is used by a great many in mixing vegetable oils, such as linseed, etc. In the matter of the adulteration of oils, my experience has shown me that firms carry the adulteration just as far as their consciences will permit them. There is no set rule to follow.

Recipe No. 37

How to Arrange Catch Basins so as to Avoid Loss of Grease in Washing Floors

RECIPE NO. 37

HOW TO ARRANGE CATCH-BASINS
SO AS TO AVOID LOSS OF GREASE
IN WASHING FLOORS

Have one large tank built, and set it in the ground, allowing everything from the floors to be washed into it.   This tank is to be arranged as shown in the following cut.

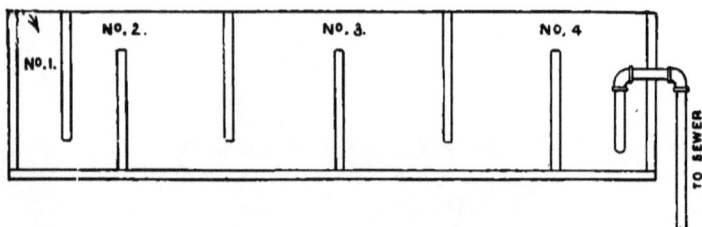

Into No. 1 everything runs; the water will run under the trap into No. 2; over No. 2 into the next compartment, etc., etc., until it reaches the last space; here it runs up through a 2-inch pipe, set in so that it only goes within 2 inches of the bottom of the tank; the grease, being the lighter, will always be on top of the water, and will almost always be found in the first and second sections.   Should some of it, however, get out, it will positively be caught in the other sections, and it is impossible for any grease to get out of the tank by this arrangement.

Recipe No. 38

Free Acid Tests

RECIPE NO. 38

FREE ACID TESTS

For these tests use an 8-ounce bottle; put in it 2 ounces of alcohol; add a few drops of tamarick (tamarisk) to color the solution. It should color the alcohol red. Place the bottle in hot water and heat it to about 150 degrees Fahrenheit, and then add to this alcohol 10 cubic centimeters of the oil to be treated. Shake well. The mixture should now be yellow. Take from a burette a caustic potash solution, and run it very slowly from the burette into this 8-ounce bottle; it must get into the mixture drop by drop, shaking well after every few drops, until it turns red—a nice cherry red—which color must remain permanent. Now look at the burette and read off how many cubic centimeters of the caustic potash solution it took to cause this reaction. Divide the figure by two and you will have the percentage of free acid in the article being tested. Now, at the first reading, it seems as if only a chemist could do this properly, but let me say that the operation is as simple as it is important.

All you have to do is to go to a chemist or to a drug store and tell them that you want two quarts of 95 degrees alcohol, to which an eighth ounce of dry carbonate of soda has been added, and that you want also one quart of caustic potash solution of sufficient strength to allow $31\frac{1}{2}$ cubic centimeters of it to exactly neutralize 5 cubic centimeters of the above mixture of acid, sulphuric and water, which contains 49 milligrams, or 1.2504 per cubic centimeter.   This will give you the solution to work with.

Buy one PIPETTE of 10 cubic centimeters, one BURETTE of 30 c.c., and 2 ounces of tamarick.

You take all this to your office and begin making your test. Take an 8-ounce bottle.   Into this put 2 ounces of the alcohol; you then place this in hot water or hold it over a spirit lamp and heat it to about 150 degrees Fahrenheit, or until it feels warm to your hand; next you heat the oil to be treated to about the same temperature.   You put your pipette into this oil and suck up to the mark 10 c. c. on the pipette; when you have reached it exactly, put your finger on the end you had in your mouth and this will prevent the oil from running out.   Look at it carefully and if there is not enough put in more; if there is too much, let the surplus drop back into the oil until the pipette marks exactly 10 c. c.

When you have got this, put the other end into the 8-ounce bottle containing the alcohol and tamarick, remembering that the 2 ounces alcohol must receive from ten to fifteen drops of tamarick to color it.   I generally use this amount to color the alcohol.

Now you let this oil run into the alcohol and tamarick mixture.   Shake it well and it will turn out a nice, bright yellow. Now you take your burette into which you have put the caustic potash preparation.   The burette is marked off in tenths—mark where you start.   Suppose it shows 30 c. c. of potash.   You allow a few drops of this to pass into the 8-ounce bottle with the oil, alcohol and tamarick solution.   Shake it well; if it does not remain a bright cherry red put in a few more drops, shaking the bottle continually until the mixture remains a bright cherry red.   This then finishes the process.

You then look at your burette and find out how many cubic

centimeters of the potash solution have been used. If you used 4 c. c., divide this by 2 and your oil will be known to contain 2 per cent of free acid. If you have used 6 c. c. of the potash solution, your oil contains 3 per cent of free acid, and so on.

A good lard oil should not run over 2 per cent of free acid, and some will go as low down as 1 per cent. Other oils run higher, some as high as 20 per cent of free acid, but these are termed No. 2 and No. 3 lard oils.

Recipe No. 39

Chemical Analysis and Properties of the
Best Fuller's Earth

RECIPE NO. 39
CHEMICAL ANALYSIS AND
PROPERTIES OF THE BEST
FULLER'S EARTH

The best brands of fuller's earth should contain but little calcium or lime.   The average analysis of fuller's earth, as given in chemistry books, is

> 65 per cent Silica
> 20 per cent Alumina
> 9 per cent Iron
> Balance Calcium and Lime
> Total, 100 per cent.

Fuller's earth is not a standard preparation, and may vary considerably in its elements and still do the work, although calcium and lime should not exist in any large amount.   Samples of fuller's earth have been handed me for examination, and I have found considerable proportions of lime and calcium contained in some of them, under the form of carbonates, which give birth very rapidly to quantities of carbonic acid when in contact with acids.

Recipe No. 40

Delicate Method of Obtaining the Percentage
of Stearic Acid or Oleic Acid
Contained in Tallow
Greases, etc.

RECIPE NO. 40
DELICATE METHOD OF OBTAINING
THE PERCENTAGE OF
STEARIC ACID OR OLEIC ACID CONTAINED
IN TALLOW, GREASES, ETC.

The following process is the one used in most laboratories. It is not a difficult one, but must be closely carried out as directed. As most of the tallow is now bought and paid for according to the percentage of stearic acid it contains, it is important to know how to make a test.

Good, fine tallow will contain the following proportions:

        45 per cent Stearic Acid
        45 per cent Oleine Oil, or Red Oil
         8 per cent Glycerine
         <u>2 per cent lost in manufacturing</u>
      100 per cent.

To test tallow so as to ascertain the point of crystallization or solidification, THE FOLLOWING APPARATUS AND SUBSTANCES are needed:

1ST. A suitable vessel, basin-shaped, and capable of holding about 2 quarts or 2 liters of liquid. A copper vessel preferred, but it must be of such material as will resist the chemical action of acids.

Suitable means of heating the above must be procured.

2D. A pair of scales is needed, capable of weighing 50 grams of tallow, or a pipette capable of measuring said quantity.

3D. A graduated glass is to be used, capable of measuring from 1 to 60 cubic centimeters.

4TH. We need, besides, a pipette of about 1 to 200 cubic centimeter capacity, with rubber ball attached for sucking up liquid from the solution of water and fatty acid.

5TH. Also a thermometer of the finest grade, capable of registering up to 100 degrees Centigrade or 500 degrees Fahrenheit each degree being divided into fifths and tenths.

6th. One half-dozen test tubes about 5 inches long and about three-fourths to seven-eighths of an inch in diameter,

7TH. A frame of iron or wood, or of any suitable material, for suspending the thermometer over and into one of the test-tubes; the latter is to be held in position by a bottle of suitable size by means of a hole cut in a cork, as shown in the illustration herein inserted.

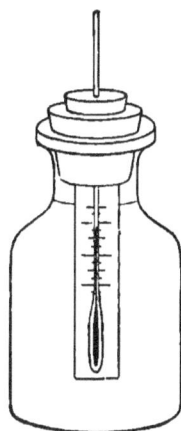

8TH. About 2 quarts of caustic soda, a solution of 36 degrees Beaume strength; about 2 quarts of sulphuric acid, a solution of 36 degrees Beaume strength; about 2 quarts of alcohoi.

9TH. A glass rod for stirring.

Here is the TESTING OPERATION:

Weigh or measure 50 grams of the sample of tallow to be tested, and heat it in the vessel until it begins to smoke. But care must be used not to allow it to burn.

Now add 40 cubic centimeters of the caustic soda solution, and 35 cubic centimeters of alcohol. Stir this until it forms into a paste, then add slowly about one quart of boiling water, and boil until thoroughly saponified, an operation which will take but a few minutes. Then pour in a little cold water to cool the solution, and boil until it becomes perfectly clear and the fatty acid separates from the soap. This last operation will occupy one hour—more or less.

The water must now be drawn off by means of a pipette, and a sufficient quantity of the fat remaining, or of the fatty acids, be put into one of the test-tubes and suspended in a bottle by means of a cork with a hole cut in, and fitted into the neck of said bottle as shown in drawing.

Place the bulb of the thermometer into one of the test-tubes, and see that the bulb is entirely covered by the liquid fatty acids, as near the center as possible.

The thermometer must be suspended so as to swing freely from the frame of iron or wood. The temperature of the fatty acid should be sufficiently high to secure a complete liquefaction at, say about 55 to 70 degrees Centigrade

Watch the thermometer carefully: it can be read accurately

by means of a small magnifying glass. As the mercury descends and finally approaches the point of crystallization, it will move more slowly and finally stop.

After a while it will rise. As soon as it stops falling and crystals begin to appear around the bulb, stir with the bulb of the thermometer the matter inside the tube, three or four times to the right and as many times to the left, then let it stand in the tube as near the center as possible, and begin watching more closely than ever.

The mercury in the thermometer will rise steadily, and the highest point it reaches is the crystallization point. The thermometer should be protected against currents of air and kept perfectly still.

Recipe No. 41

How to Cool a Meat Market with Brine Circulation

RECIPE NO. 41

HOW TO COOL A MEAT MARKET

WITH BRINE CIRCULATION

Here is a nice and economical way of keeping your market fairly cool:

Have plenty of 1¼ inch pipe placed about 6 or 7 feet above the level of your floor. Have ABOVE this floor, a large tank built and well insulated; in this tank place your ice and salt, keeping the tank well covered. This will reduce the temperature of the water to 32 degrees Fahrenheit; then open a valve and let this water flow through your pipes and run into a tank built UNDER your floor.

This second tank, of course, must also be well insulated and so arranged that ice and salt can be put into it; then a pump is arranged in connection with this tank, and the same water is pumped back, upstairs, into Tank No. 1. If you keep the doors of your store closed and use a little care, you can keep your temperature down to 55 or 60 degrees Fahrenheit, in hot weather, and do so very cheaply. Of course the temperature can be brought down even lower by using more ice and salt and plenty of iron piping, and by insulating your shop thoroughly.

Here is the way the apparatus should be arranged:

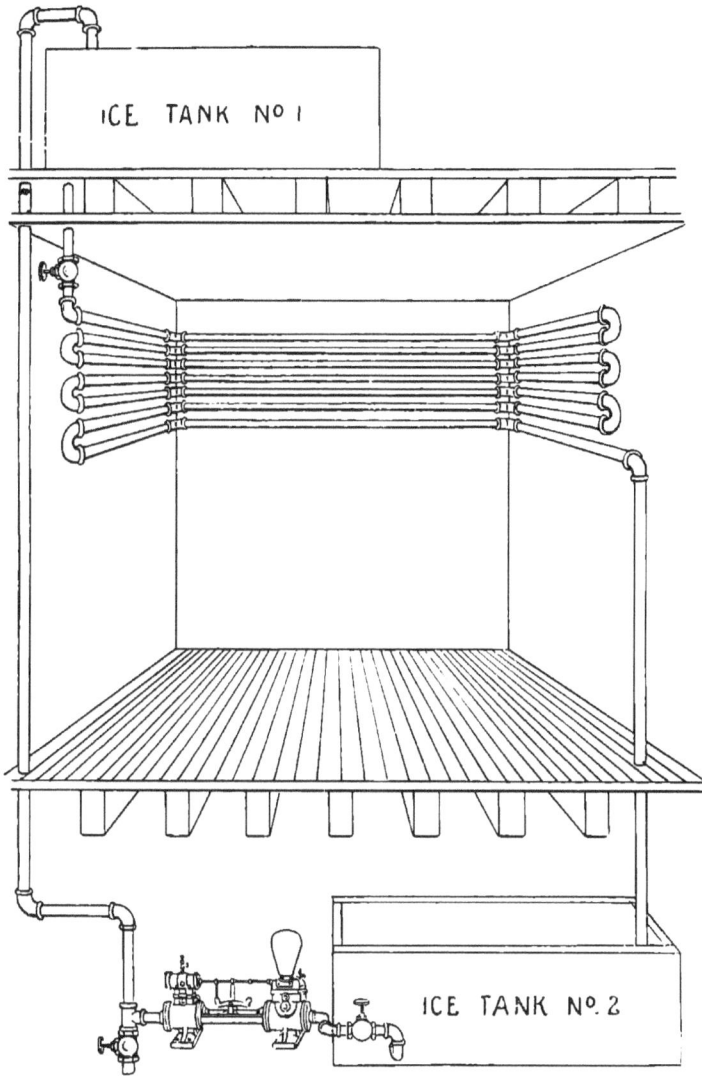

ICE TANK Nº 1

ICE TANK Nº 2

Recipe No. 42

How to Keep and Use a Chill-Room to Best Advantage

RECIPE NO. 42
HOW TO KEEP
AND USE A CHILL-ROOM
TO BEST ADVANTAGE

A chill-room should be filled every alternate day.

Hogs are to hang 40 to 43 hours and cattle the same.

Hogs should hang in a temperature of 32 degrees Fahrenheit.

Cattle should hang in a temperature of 38 degrees Fahrenheit.

Hogs averaging 200 to 250 lbs. require, each, 3½ sq. ft. of space.

Cattle of 800 lbs. dressed, require, each, from 10 to 12 sq. ft. of space.

To chill 1,000 hogs and 300 cattle will require a machine of 100 tons refrigerating capacity; storage will take besides 40 to 50 tons; you therefore need two machines of 80 tons each, and they will cost you, complete, about $40,000.

In figuring what storage is required, always figure 8,000 to 12,000 cubic feet per ton refrigerator.

Recipe No. 43

How to Properly Fit Up a Test Room

RECIPE NO. 43
HOW TO PROPERLY FIT UP
A TEST ROOM

Every lard refinery or packing house should fit up a small room, kept under lock and key, for making tests etc. In this room should be made all tests of lards, tallows, oils, greases, etc. You need no professional chemist for those tests. You can very easily learn how to make yourselves the few, occasional tests our business may require.

To fit up your little laboratory, go to any chemical supply shop and purchase:

                3 12-ounce beakers
                1 dozen 8-ounce bottles
                1 10-c. c. pipette
                2 glass funnels, 6 inches diameter
                2 8-ounce wash-bottles
                1 porcelain mortar and pestle of 4 inches diameter
                1 Bunsen gas-lamp, plain
                1 glass spatula, 6 inches long
                1 iron ring stand
                2 dozen test-tubes, 6 inches by ⅜ inch
                1 tube rack of 12 holes
                1 chemical thermometer, 600 degrees Fahrenheit
                3 evaporators of porcelain, 6 inches in diameter

3 evaporators of porcelain, 12 inches in diameter
1 package filter paper, 12 inches in diameter
2 rings for filter-stands
1 small tincture press.

These articles will cost but a trifle, and they will be sufficient for making a number of tests.

Recipe No. 44

How to Use and Compare the Different Scales of Thermometers

185

RECIPE NO. 44
HOW TO USE, AND COMPARE
THE DIFFERENT SCALES
OF THERMOMETERS

When using thermometers, much annoyance has been caused by the existence of the three different scales in use in the different civilized countries of the world.

The REAUMUR SCALE prevails in Germany.

The CENTIGRADE (or Celsius) SCALE, in France and generally wherever the metric system of weights and measures is followed, and in all, except English-speaking countries, for every scientific purpose.

The FAHRENHEIT SCALE, in the United States and the British Empire.

The best argument in favor of the CENTIGRADE SCALE is that it includes between its 0 degree (freezing point of water) and 100 degrees (boiling point of water) all the temperatures generally met with in the civilized zone.

The FAHRENHEIT SCALE is convenient on account of its short degrees, of which there are 180 between the freezing point of water (32 degrees) and the boiling point of water (212 degrees), thus allowing more minute calculations without the use of fractions. Its low zero makes it possible, in temperate climates, to dispense with the sign − .

The REAUMUR SCALE divides the space between the freezing and boiling of water into 80 degrees, instead of 100 degrees, as in the centigrade system.

The conversion of any one of these scales into another is very simple. You just proceed as follows:

1ST. To convert a temperature given by a Fahrenheit scale into one given by a centigrade scale, subtract 32 from the figure on the Fahrenheit thermometer, multiply the remainder by 5 and divide by 9. The product will give you the same temperature in centigrade degrees.

2D. To convert Fahrenheit degrees into Reaumur degrees, subtract 32, multiply by 4 and divide by 9. The product gives you the same temperature according to the Reaumur scale.

3D. To convert centigrade degrees into Fahrenheit degrees, multiply the centigrade temperature by 9 and divide by 5, adding 32 to the result. You will then have the same temperature expressed in Fahrenheit degrees.

4TH. To convert Reaumur degrees into Fahrenheit degrees, multiply the Reaumur temperature by 9 and divide by 4, adding 32 to the result. You'll have the same temperature expressed in Fahrenheit degrees.

The following is a table giving equivalents in Centigrade, Reaumur and Fahrenheit degrees up to the boiling point of water, prepared for the convenience of those who do not care to take the trouble of converting temperatures from one scale into another.

COMPARISONS BETWEEN CENTIGRADE, REAUMUR AND FAHRENHEIT SCALES

C.	R.	F.	C.	R.	F.
−30	−24.0	−22.0	−1	−0.8	30.2
−29	−23.0	−20.2	0	0.0	32.0
−28	−22.4	−18.4	1	0.8	33.8
−27	−21.6	−16.6	2	1.6	35.6
−26	−20.8	−14.8	3	2.4	37.4
−25	−20.0	−13.0	4	3.2	39.2
−24	−19.2	−11.2	5	4.0	41.0
−23	−18.4	−9.4	6	4.8	42.8
−22	−17.6	−7.6	7	5.6	44.6
−21	−16.8	−5.8	8	6.4	46.4
−20	−16.0	−4.0	9	7.2	48.2
−19	−15.2	−2.2	10	8.0	50.0
−18	−14.4	−0.4	11	8.8	51.8
−17	−13.6	1.4	12	9.6	53.6
−16	−12.8	3.2	13	10.4	55.4
−15	−12.0	5.0	14	11.2	57.2
−14	−11.2	6.8	15	12.0	59.0
−13	−10.4	8.6	16	12.8	60.8
−12	−9.6	10.4	17	13.6	62.6
−11	−8.8	12.2	18	14.4	64.4
−10	−8.0	14.0	19	15.2	66.2
−9	−7.2	15.8	20	16.0	68.0
−8	−6.4	17.6	21	16.8	69.8
−7	−5.6	19.4	22	17.6	71.6
−6	−4.8	21.2	23	18.4	73.4
−5	−4.0	23.0	24	19.2	75.2
−4	−3.2	24.8	25	20.0	77.0
−3	−2.4	26.6	26	20.8	78.8
−2	−1.6	28.4	27	21.6	80.6

COMPARISONS BETWEEN
CENTIGRADE, REAUMUR AND FAHRENHEIT
SCALES

C.	R.	F.	C.	R.	F
28	22.4	82.4	65	52.0	149.0
29	23.2	84.2	66	52.8	150.8
30	24.0	86.0	67	53.6	152.6
31	24.8	87.8	68	54.4	154.4
32	25.6	89.6	69	55.2	156.2
33	26.4	91.4	70	56.0	158.0
34	27.2	93.2	71	56.8	159.8
35	28.0	95.0	72	57.6	161.6
36	28.8	96.8	73	58.4	163.4
37	29.6	98.6	74	59.2	165.2
38	30.4	100.4	75	60.0	167.0
39	31.2	102.2	76	60.8	168.8
40	32.0	104.4	77	61.6	170.6
41	32.8	105.8	78	62.4	172.4
42	33.6	107.6	79	63.2	174.2
43	34.4	109.4	80	64.0	176.0
44	35.2	111.2	81	64.8	177.8
45	36.0	113.0	82	65.6	179.6
46	36.8	114.8	83	66.4	181.4
47	37.6	116.6	84	67.2	183.2
48	38.4	118.4	85	68.0	185.0
49	39.2	120.2	86	68.8	186.8
50	40.0	122.0	87	69.6	188.6
51	40.8	123.8	88	70.4	190.4
52	41.6	125.6	89	71.2	192.2
53	42.4	127.4	90	72.0	194.0
54	43.2	129.2	91	72.8	195.8
55	44.0	131.0	92	73.6	197.6
56	44.8	132.8	93	74.4	199.4
57	45.6	134.6	94	75.2	201.2
58	46.4	136.4	95	76.0	203.0
59	47.2	138.2	96	76.8	204.8
60	48.0	140.0	97	77.6	206.6
61	48.8	141.8	98	78.4	208.4
62	49.6	143.6	99	79.2	210.2
63	50.4	145.4	100	80.0	212.0
64	51.2	147.2			

Recipe No. 45

Specifications for Lard Oil

191

RECIPE NO. 45

SPECIFICATIONS FOR LARD OIL

Two grades of lard oil, known on the market as "Extra" and 'Extra No. 1," are used, the former principally for burning, the other as a lubricant.   The material desired under specifications is oil pressed from the lard of corn-fed hogs, unmixed with other oils and containing the least possible amount of free acid.   Also, from October 1st to May 1st it should show a cold test of not higher than 43 degrees Fahrenheit.   Oil from lard of "mash" or distillery-fed hogs does not give good results in service and should never be sent to railroads.   Also care should be observed to have the oil made from fresh lard; old lard gives an oil that does not burn well and also works badly as a lubricant.   Whenever pressing lard always figure 15c per 100 lbs. for labor.

The use of the so-called "neatsfoot stock," either alone or as an admixture in making the "Extra No. 1" grade, is not recommended.   Neatsfoot oil is used by the railroad companies when the price will admit, but it is always preferred unmixed.   Both grades of oil will be purchased on sample and shipments must conform to sample.   A 4-ounce sample is sufficient and should be sent to the purchasing agent of the road; the color of the sample has an influence in the securing of orders; the lightest in color are always considered the best.   Shipments must be made as soon as possible after the order is placed.   All shipments received at any shop after October 1st will be subject to cold tests and rejected if they fail, unless it can be shown that the shipment has been more than a week in transit.

The EXTRA grade will not be accepted when

1ST. It contains admixtures of any other oils.

2D. It contains more free acid than is neutralized by 4 c.c. of alkali, as described.

3D. It shows a cold test above 45 degrees Fahrenheit from October 1 to May 1.

A shipment of EXTRA No. 1 will not be accepted when

1ST. It contains admixtures of any other oils.

2D. It contains more free acid than is neutralized by 30 c.c of alkali.

3D. It shows a cold test above 45 degrees Fahrenheit from October 1 to May 1.

Recipe No. 46

Pure Neatsfoot Oil

RECIPE NO. 46
PURE NEATSFOOT OIL

This oil is made from the feet only, by heating just below boiling point.

Then the feet are taken and screened; this throws out the meat, etc. This meat is then boiled thoroughly and allowed to settle, when the stock is carefully skimmed, and this oil makes a No. 1 neatsfoot oil.

Now, if this oil is taken and filtered, the floating stearine will be caught. It then sells for an extra oil. The stearine can be put into the tallow-tank and used for tallow.

The head stock oil is refined and an A No. 1 oil made by pressing this stearine as it goes into the tallow-tank.

Recipe No. 47

Cold Test of Lard Oils

RECIPE NO. 47
COLD TEST OF LARD OILS

This test is made as follows:

A couple of ounces of oil are put in a 4-ounce sample
bottle and a thermometer introduced in it.   The oil is then
frozen, a freezing mixture of ice and salt being used if necessary.
When the oil has become hard, the bottle is removed from the
freezing mixture and the frozen oil allowed to soften, being stirred
and well mixed at the same time, by means of the thermometer,
until the mass will run from one end of the bottle to the other.

The reading of the thermometer, when this operation has
been gone through, is regarded as the cold test of the oil.   .

We have treated in our Recipe No. 38, under the heading
of FREE ACID TESTS, all that concerns this important
analysis.

Specification

Issued by the Penn. R. R. Company
Power Department

SPECIFICATION ISSUED BY THE
PENN. R. R. COMPANY
POWER DEPARTMENT

"From this date all materials used as lubricants and burning oils will be purchased by weight, and quotation of prices and bills must be by the pound and not gallons. In quoting prices cents and 100ths should be used. A separate bill must be rendered for every shipment, however small, even though it be but a portion of the whole order; and the bill must be made as soon as possible after the shipment is made.

"Every package containing lubricants and burning oils must be plainly marked with the gross weight and tare.

"This applies to oil-tank cars as well as to barrels.

"Parties failing to mark both gross and tare on their packages must accept the company's weights without any question.

"Whenever a shipment of any lubricant or burning oil is received at any point, it will be immediately weighed and, when practicable, will be at once emptied and the empty packages weighed. If not practicable to empty all the packages, 5 per cent of the shipment will be emptied and the tares taken of the whole. The tares of the whole shipment will then be adjusted in accordance with the weight of the 5 per cent; if the net weight found from above data is less than the amount charged for in the bill by more than 1 per cent, a deduction will be made from the bill equal to the amount of deficiency over 1 per cent.

"This 1 per cent covers leakage in transit and the amount which adheres to the barrels when emptying them, also possible slight difference in scales."

Analysis

Of Prime Winter=Strained Lard Oil

ANALYSIS OF PRIME
WINTER-STRAINED LARD OIL

Prime, winter-strained lard oil contains less than 2 per cent of free acids, for the cold test must stand a temperature of 45 degrees Fahrenheit or less.

Its specific gravity is 22 to 24 degrees Beaume. at a temperature of 60 degrees Fahrenheit.

Sundry Recommendations

Concerning Extra Winter-
Strained Lard
Oil

SUNDRY RECOMMENDATIONS
CONCERNING EXTRA WINTER-STRAINED
LARD OIL

In pressing stock to obtain E. W. S. (i. e., Extra Winter-Strained Lard Oil), always press from the choicest prime steam lard.   There is always a good demand for the oil and stearine.

Press it in winter, on account of the cold temperature; in summer, if you have refrigerating facilities to keep the press-room cold, always make a test of your lard by pressing a small quantity in your laboratory in your tincture-press.

Make an acid test of your oil; this you can do by following directions under heading of FREE ACID TESTS. If your oil shows OVER 2 per cent of acid, there is no use pressing it out of the lard you are just then working from, and expecting it to pass for an E. W. S. lard oil, as it is sure to be rejected.   But if it shows 2 per cent of acid or LESS, press it and you will have no trouble getting top price for both oil and stearine.

Recipe No. 48

How to Detect Water and Impurities

RECIPE NO. 48

HOW TO DETECT WATER

AND IMPURITIES

WATER. Weigh carefully and exactly 20 grams of the article to be tested in a small porcelain dish; then place the latter over an alcohol stove; let it get very hot WITHOUT BURNING it; when small bubbles cease coming to the top, reweigh, and the loss in weight will give you the percentage of water.

IMPURITIES. Now take the material in a dish, and, after carefully weighing two filter papers against each other, add some naphtha to the material and pass the whole through one of the filter papers. Carefully wash all grease out of filter paper with warm naphtha, using a wash bottle. Weigh the two papers against each other again; the increased weight gained by the one you used for the above operation gives you the percentage of impurities. An oven may be used instead of an alcohol stove. Do not heat above 180 degrees Fahrenheit.

Recipe No. 49

Making Sweet Pickle for Curing Meats

Hams

RECIPE NO. 49

MAKING SWEET PICKLE

FOR CURING MEATS — HAMS

One tierce of 16-lb. hams contains about 16 to 19 pieces.
In packing these, put into the tierce with the hams

18 ozs. Saltpeter
4 lbs. Granulated Sugar.

Then fill the tierce up with 85 degrees proof pickle for a
mild cure.

It will take these hams 85 to 90 days to become cured.

When first packed they will weigh about 300 lbs.   When
taken out they will weigh about 322 lbs.

These hams should be kept in a temperature not over 38
degrees Fahrenheit and should be rolled the fifth day after being packed; again on the fifteenth day; then again on the thirtieth
day; then allow them to rest.   The object in rolling them is to
find the cripples and leakers; also to evenly mix the ingredients
and also to get the pickle into the hams that might partly be dry.
Should you find leakers, be sure and have the tierce reopened and
repickled.   Always use the same strength of pickle as was used
before.

Recipe No. 50

Dry Salting Meats

RECIPE NO. 50

DRY SALTING MEATS

Use Ashten salt.

Get ready a barrel full of 100 degrees proof pickle.

Now take the meats, drop them into the pickle, take them out and put them in a salt-box and rub a little salt all over them. Then pile them cuts UP, flanks UP, sprinkle 2 ounces fine saltpeter over the pile; shake a small handful of salt on top.

In packing hams lay them left and right in order to allow the pickle to run down the stifle joint, then, in five days, overhaul them in a box.

Always try to save the pickle that these hams make and use this pickle on the hams again, then rub them slightly with salt and lay them on a pile. In about 10 days overhaul them again. If your temperature is steady, at, say from 36 to 38 degrees, you can let them stay fifteen days. Use fine salt again when overhauling them. You will find they have a fine cherry color, which suits the English market. They are ready to pack any time after the 25th day, as they cure in shipment.

Recipe No. 51

Points of Interest about Hams

RECIPE NO. 51
POINTS OF INTEREST
ABOUT HAMS

In making hams, 12 to 14-lb. hams are worth more than hams 16 to 18 lbs.

Be sure to always save the pickle these hams make, as no pickle can be made to equal it.

Light, long clears, 35 to 40 lbs.

Cumberland light, about 32 lbs; heavy, 35 to 40 lbs.

Birmingham sides, light, about 35 to 40 lbs.

Yorkshire, 40 to 45 lbs.

Long ribs, light, about 18 to 20 lbs; heavy, 20 to 25 lbs.

Long cut hams, light, run from 12 to 14 lbs.

Long cut hams, medium, run from 16 to 18 lbs.

Long cut hams, heavy, run from 18 to 20 lbs.

Strafford hams, about 16 to 18 lbs.

Preston hams, about 16 to 18 lbs., the left bone left on.

California hams, about 10 to 12 lbs.

Picnic hams, about 8 to 10 lbs.

Boston shoulder, about 6 to 8 lbs.

When packing hams in tierces with salt, use

21 lbs. Salt
12 ozs. Saltpeter
4 lbs. Granulated Sugar.

Fill up the tierce with water; roll it the same as in the sweet pickle process.

I would recommend using no pump in curing hams; my reason is that it does not make choice hams. One of the large Chicago houses has lost, in one season, over $30,000 by getting air into the hams, and now very few large packers use the pump. When you get a good, careful man to use this pump, you might take the risk, if you are in a hurry, as it cures the meat in 65 days. But it does not make choice hams.

Recipe No. 52

Sweet Pickle Bellies

RECIPE NO. 52
SWEET PICKLE BELLIES

The formula is the following:

> ¾ lb. Saltpeter
> 4 lbs. Granulated Sugar
> 75 lbs. Proof Pickle

They take 40 days to cure.
Roll them the same as you do hams.

Recipe No. 53

How Meat Should be Treated Before You Start Packing It

RECIPE NO. 53
HOW MEAT SHOULD BE
TREATED BEFORE YOU START
PACKING IT

Hogs, from the time they are killed, should hang 48 hours before cutting up in a temperature of 35 to 36 degrees Fahrenheit, or colder.

After cutting, hams and shoulders should be spread out on racks for 48 hours before packing, in the same temperature (35 to 36 degrees Fahrenheit, or lower). This will get all the animal heat out of them, and is the great secret in curing meats. Be sure that all the animal heat is out. THEN GO AHEAD.

Recipe No. 54

For Curing Back Pork

RECIPE NO. 54

FOR CURING BACK PORK

Take from 35 to 40 pieces; use 10 lbs. rock salt, coarse; 8 ozs. saltpeter.

Fill barrels with 90 degrees proof pickle. This will cure clear pork or back pork; this sells for either family pork or back pork, and can be branded as such.

Cut this square and uniform.

A short rib about 35 to 40 average makes back and belly. Put the back into backs or family pork, and the bellies go for sweet pickled bellies.

Shoulders should be cut off with two ribs left on the square

Recipe No. 55

Bellies

RECIPE NO. 55
BELLIES

On an 8 or 10-lb. average belly, leave the rib in.

On clear belly, 10 or 12 lbs., take the rib out. You can make these 12 to 14 lbs., according to your trade. Heavy bellies can be sold 12 to 14 lbs. average, and light ones from 10 to 12 lbs. average. Light bellies are always worth more than heavy ones.

In making a choice belly, always be sure to cut the seed out. What is meant by seed is this: A sow pig, after she loses her young, dries up, and the milk goes into what is called the seed. This is very objectionable when making a sale, and will not pass inspection.

Recipe No. 56

What Constitutes Prime Mess Pork

RECIPE NO. 56
WHAT CONSTITUTES
PRIME MESS PORK

This is cut from the whole side, except ham, which is taken off first. Then split the side right through the middle. Chop shank and foot off.

Now take the back and cut it into four pieces up to the blade. Make two pieces out of the balance.

Then chop flank square; make 4-lb. pieces up to the shank; if the other is over 6 lbs., cut it in two parts. Otherwise let it go as one.

A barrel of prime mess pork contains

20 pieces Coarse
30 pieces Prime.

The prime is made up to the blade, and the bellies up to the shank. The prime pieces must weigh 115 lbs., and the coarse, 75 lbs. When taken out the whole will weigh 310 lbs., 40 days old.

In packing, use a little fine salt between each layer, and 6 ozs. saltpeter, with 10 lbs. coarse salt, and fill the barrel up with 90 degrees proof pickle.

In following up this process you can rely upon getting a fine color and choice goods. In making prime mess pork take about 40 average, or between 35 and 40. Leave the shoulder on and split through the middle.

Recipe No. 57

Mess Pork

225

RECIPE NO. 57
MESS PORK

In making mess pork, the ham and shoulder should be cut from the side; in cutting the shoulder off, cut the butt narrow, then cut pieces from 5½ to 6½ inches wide. On the flank, cut square pieces.

In packing mess pork, say twelve pieces to the barrel, it will take three sides. Pack two shoulders in the bottom of the barrel; one flank, then one shoulder; two middles; and always save three good pieces for header.

Pack the balance in the third row.

Use 20 lbs. fine salt; 20 lbs. coarse salt.

Put one-third coarse in the bottom of the barrel; mix fine salt between the pork and put two-thirds coarse salt on top. Fill the barrel with water, or you may use 20 lbs. coarse salt, and fill with pickle 100 degrees proof. But I think that using salt will give best satisfaction.

Pack 290 lbs. to the barrel; this must be EXACT. In about six months this will weigh 306 lbs., which is regular. If older, it will weigh from 315 to 318 lbs.

Break this down twice. First, after 10 days; second, after 20 days.

If cutting heavy pieces, 10 pieces are worth more than 12 pieces. A premium of 25 cents per barrel is always paid for 10 pieces in preference to 12 pieces. Twelve pieces are worth more than 14 pieces. But do not go over 14 pieces to the barrel, as it will not be regular if you do.

Recipe No. 58

Light Long Clears

RECIPE NO. 58
LIGHT LONG CLEARS

Light long clears must be cut square; the backbone must be taken off and the ribs taken out, the slip-bone sawed down even with the meat.

Long cut hams are cut from long cut clears that would leave no split bone, and, consequently, would need no sawing. The blade should be taken out with a small pocket, and the shoulder bone should be taken out with the shank and side. Leaf lard should be scraped clean out of the belly, and cut square at each end. You can use the same cure as is used in curing long cut hams.

Recipe No. 59

Cumberland Cuts

RECIPE NO. 59

CUMBERLAND CUTS

The backbone should be sawed off, one rib taken off, shoulder with neck bone, foot cut off at second joint.

Clean out the belly and cut the end square.

These cuts must be free from seed and old sows. They must strictly come from choice hogs. The cure for them is the same as for long cut hams and clears.

They should be cured by dipping in pickle and then put in a box and rubbed lightly with salt. Put most of the salt on the back and shoulder, as these are the thickest parts to be cured.

Use 2 ounces saltpeter on each side; pile them eight high. It takes 15 to 20 days before they are ready for shipment. Overhaul them in 5 days, and again in 10 days. Do not salt this meat too heavily.

In packing this meat for shipment, put a layer of salt, about one inch thick, in the bottom; then rub the cuts through a box and sprinkle a handful of salt on shoulder and back. On the top side of box put a good layer of salt, and turn the skin side up. The box will weigh between 490 and 510 lbs.

Recipe No. 60

Birmingham Sides

RECIPE NO. 60

BIRMINGHAM SIDES

They are cured the same as Cumberland and Long Clear. They are as follows:

Saw the backbone off and take ribs out, then raise the blade bone; make a saucer pocket: cut shank off at joint close to the breast: then take a thin slice of lean meat off the back and cut end square.

Recipe No. 61

Yorkshire Cuts

RECIPE NO. 61
YORKSHIRE CUTS

The backbone and ribs being out, cut the shank about one inch above the first joint and square the ends.   Always use the thickest backs for Yorkshire cuts and use the others for Cumberlands and Birminghams.

Recipe No. 62

Long Rib Cuts

RECIPE NO. 62
LONG RIB CUTS

Saw the backbone and take out one rib with the neck bone and the blade bone; but make a small pocket and twist the shoulder bone out with the shank.

Recipe No. 63

Strafford Hams

RECIPE NO. 63
STRAFFORD HAMS

These should be cut about 2 inches from the lift bone, and in trimming leave the fat full.   Take the lift bone off at joint; saw the foot about 1 inch from hock.

Recipe No. 64

Preston Cuts

RECIPE NO 64
PRESTON CUTS

Cut in the same manner as for Strafford ham, only leave the left bone on.

Recipe No. 65

California Hams

RECIPE NO. 65

CALIFORNIA HAMS

This shoulder should weigh 18 to 20 lbs. and be cut one inch from the joint; this takes the butt off; trim it round.

In this cut there is a lop of lean meat; this is over the blade.

Lift this up and cut it and the blob fat off.   That makes the California ham look lean and is just what is wanted.   Cut shank off to expose the marrow about 1½ inches above first joint.

Recipe No. 66

Picnic Hams

RECIPE NO. 66
PICNIC HAMS

They are made according to the preceding recipe, except that lighter hogs are used.

Recipe No. 67

Boston Shoulder

RECIPE NO. 67
BOSTON SHOULDER

Cut close to the joint, NOT INTO IT, for if you cut into it the bone shows too large

IN PACKING BACK PORK

Use iron bound barrels, that is barrels with one iron hoop at each end.

Recipe No. 68

Short Clears Packed for Export

.

RECIPE NO. 68
SHORT CLEARS PACKED
FOR EXPORT

These are made from heavy hogs, from 7 to 9 pieces and from 8 to 10 pieces per barrel

These are cut exactly like short ribs, only the backbone is taken out and cleared. These are cured in American salt, no saltpeter being used.

Recipe No. 69

Extra Short Cuts

RECIPE NO. 69
EXTRA SHORT CUTS

These are made from lighter hogs, 35 to 45 average.   Scribe
the rib with a saw just even to the meat; this makes a line of pork.
Cure this in the same manner as short clears.   The great demand
for these comes from the South.

Recipe No. 70

Short Ribs

RECIPE NO. 70
SHORT RIBS

Raise the backbone and saw it off; take tenderloins out, scrape leaf lard out, and cure the same as long clears.

Packers generally figure one day to the pound for cure thus a 40-lb. piece would take about 40 days, etc.

Recipe No. 71

Three Rib Shoulder

RECIPE NO. 71

THREE RIB SHOULDER

This is cut from the side, between the third and fourth rib; that leaves three ribs on the shoulder. Then raise the ribs and neck bone off, but leave all the meat on the shoulder; it must be smooth. Trim all the blood off the neck and cut even with the lean meat. Saw off the foot above the first joint, square.

Cure the same as you do long cuts.

For export have these cuts uniform, averaging 15 to 17 lbs

Recipe No. 72

Food for Stock

RECIPE NO. 72

FOOD FOR STOCK

The following table shows the number of pounds of various products, used as food for stock, which are equivalent in value to 10 pounds of hay.

FOOD	LBS.
Barley	5 to 6
Cabbage	20 to 30
Carrots, red	25 to 30
Carrots, white	40 to 45
Clover, green	40 to 50
Indian corn	5 to 7
Mangel-wurzel	30 to 35
Oats	4 to 7
Oil-cake	2 to 4
Peas and beans	3 to 5
Potatoes	20 to 25
Barley straw	20 to 40
Oat straw	20 to 40
Pea straw	10 to 15
Wheat straw	40 to 50

Recipe No. 73

Table of Corn, What it Will Produce
in Pork

RECIPE NO. 73
TABLE OF CORN, WHAT IT
WILL PRODUCE IN PORK

One bushel of corn will make 10½ lbs. of pork, gross.

With Corn at 12½ cents per bushel, Pork costs 1½ cents per lb.
With Corn at 17 cents per bushel, Pork costs 2 cents per lb.
With Corn at 25 cents per bushel, Pork costs 3 cents per lb.
With Corn at 35 cents per bushel, Pork costs 4 cents per lb
With Corn at 42 cents per bushel, Pork costs 5 cents per lb.
With Corn at 50 cents per bushel, Pork costs 6 cents per lb.

Recipe No. 74

Food for Sheep

RECIPE NO. 74
FOOD FOR SHEEP

The following table shows the number of pounds, live weight, and the number of pounds of wool and of tallow produced by 1,000 lbs. of each of the articles named, when used as food for sheep:

Kind of Food	Increase in Weight Pounds	Wool Produced Pounds	Tallow Produced Pounds
Barley	136	11½	60
Buckwheat	120	10	33
Corn Meal, wet	129	13½	17½
Mangel-wurzel, raw	38½	5¼	6½
Oats	146	10	42½
Peas	134	14½	41
Potatoes, raw, with salt	46½	6½	12½
Potatoes, raw, without salt	44	6½	11½
Rye, with salt	133	14	35
Rye, without salt	90	12	43
Wheat	155	14	59½

Facts and Advice

For Building Packing Houses

FACTS AND ADVICE FOR
BUILDING PACKING HOUSES

One-fifth more siding and flooring is needed than the number of square feet of surface to be covered, on account of the lap in siding and matching of flooring.

A cord of stone, 3 bushels of lime and 1 cubic yard of sand will lay 100 cubic feet of wall.

Twenty-two cubic feet of stone, when built into a wall, is one perch.

Three pecks lime and 4 bushels sand are required to each perch of wall.

There are 20 common bricks in a cubic foot when laid, and 15 common bricks to 1 foot of an 8-inch wall when laid.

Five courses of brick will lay 1 foot in height. On a chimney, 8 bricks in a course will make a flue 4 inches wide and 10 inches long.

One bushel cement and 2 bushels sand will cover $3\frac{1}{2}$ square yards 1 inch thick, or $4\frac{1}{2}$ square yards $\frac{3}{4}$ inch thick, or $6\frac{3}{4}$ square yards $\frac{1}{2}$ inch thick.

One bushel cement and 1 bushel sand will cover $2\frac{1}{4}$ square yards 1 inch thick, or 3 square yards $\frac{3}{4}$ inch thick, or $4\frac{1}{2}$ square yards $\frac{1}{2}$ inch thick.

Two thousand shingles laid 4 inches to the weather will cover 200 square feet of roof, and $10\frac{1}{2}$ lbs. of 4-penny nails will fasten them on.

PILING UP TIERCES

A great many packers, when piling up tierces, will be glad to know the amount of surface feet it will take to store 1,000 tierces piled up three high. The space will be exactly 43 feet long and 64 feet wide, or 2,750 square feet.

This allows 6 feet for alley.

Actual Statement

Taken from one of the Largest Packing Houses

263

ACTUAL STATEMENT TAKEN
FROM ONE OF THE LARGEST
PACKING HOUSES

Total number hogs killed from May 1 to April 30 (1 year): 365,376.
Amount of ice used in connection with same: 22,488,000 lbs.

    Total hogs killed in one week:

Packers	3,697
Shippers	964
Total	4,391

	LBS.
Total amount of Lard produced	178,828
Total amount of Grease produced .	9,350
Ice used per head .	. $61\frac{54}{100}$
Lard produced per head .	$40\frac{72}{100}$
Grease produced per head	$2\frac{17}{100}$
Blood produced per head .	$1\frac{50}{100}$
Tankage produced per head . .	$1\frac{75}{100}$
Prime Steam Lard produced per head	$26\frac{60}{100}$
Kettle-rendered Lard produced per head .	$13\frac{40}{100}$

The following is from actual work for six months in one of our largest packing houses.

The number of cattle killed was 290,180 head. These produced:

A. Tallow, 2,719,795 lbs.—Average per head, 9.37 lbs.
B. Tallow,   868,540 lbs.—Average per head, 2.99 lbs.
T. Tallow,   443,700 lbs. Average per head, 1.53 lbs.
Black Grease and Catch-Basin stock, 157,850 lbs.
    Average per head   .5439 lb.

ANOTHER TEST was made with the following result.
On Bone Grease:

Cattle killed	287,163 head
Yield in Skull and Jawbone Grease	238,700 lbs.
Average per head	.331 lb.
Skull Grease	58,100 lbs.
Average per head	.2023 lb.
Head Oil stock	119,350 lbs.
Average per head	.4156 lb.

TEST ON 270,234 HEAD OF SHEEP:

Yield of Mutton Tallow	440,000 lbs.
Average per head	1.64 lbs.

ANOTHER TEST ON 214,954 HOGS:

Prime Steam Lard	5,637,201 lbs.
Average per head	26.22 lbs.
Hog Grease	305,782 lbs.
Average per head	1.44 lbs.

ANOTHER ACTUAL TEST, which can be fully relied upon, gives the number of hogs killed, the percentages of cost, and products for one week:

Hogs killed	13,698
Pay-roll	$119.02
No. of lbs. per head	33
Cost of killing per head	seven-eighths cent

Prime Steam Lard	394,965 lbs.	87¾ per cent
Neutral Lard	6,480 lbs.	1½ per cent
Kettle Steam Lard	37,648 lbs.	8¼ per cent
Grease	13,500 lbs.	3 per cent
	452,293 lbs.	100 per cent

This test shows about 29 lbs. prime steam lard to the hog, and 3 lbs. leaf lard to the hog.

Cost Per Head

Of Rendering Cattle at One of the Large Packing Houses

COST PER HEAD
OF RENDERING CATTLE
AT ONE OF THE LARGE PACKING
HOUSES

Total number of Cattle rendered .	4,216
Total number of lbs. produced . .	. 55.800 lbs.
Number of lbs. produced per head	14 lbs
Cost of production .	4 cents

ANOTHER TEST shows:

Total number of Cattle rendered .	. 10,457
Total produced . .	139,300 lbs.
Produced per head	14 lbs.
Cost of production .	3¼ cents

Recipe No. 75

How to Make Candles

RECIPE NO. 75

HOW TO MAKE CANDLES

The first step is to remove the glycerine from the tallow. This is done with a digester, as previously mentioned. After the glycerine is removed, the fatty acids are treated with sulphuric acid to remove the lime. After this is done, the fatty acids, or, as it is termed, the "acid grease," is run into a room where shallow pans are placed made entirely of galvanized iron, lined or enameled to prevent the acid from destroying the metal. It is allowed to remain in this room for several days at a temperature of about 70 degrees Fahrenheit, so that it will grain properly When the fat becomes properly grained it has the appearance of maple sugar. This color comes from the oleic acid which it contains. From this room the stock is taken to the press room and wrapped in heavy woolen cloths, put in a perpendicular hydraulic press termed the "Cold Press," placed between iron plates, and pressure applied. A dark oil, called red oil, is pressed out, and is sold to soap manufacturers. The oil, being squeezed out, leaves the grease of a yellowish white. From the cold press it is taken to a horizontal press, termed a "Hot Press," and subjected to another heavy pressing. This hot press is arranged with hollow plates that are kept hot with steam-pipes, as shown in the engraving. Both the hot and cold presses, with their proper fittings and pumps, are here fully shown. The grease from the cold press is now placed in the hot press, and between each of the hollow iron plates are bags made of horse hair. The grease is placed in these, and the steam is applied to each plate and the press heated. The pumps are now started very slowly, and a heavy pressure applied. When taken from this press the grease will be found to be as white as snow, and very hard. It is now termed stearic acid. This stearic acid is now shaken out into barrels and ready to be molded for candles.

The stearic acid industry, which is now of large proportions, originated in M. Chevreul's discovery that fats are composed of one or more inflammable fatty acids combined with a comparatively uninflammable base, glycerine.

Thus tallow or palm oil consists of palmitic, stearic and oleic acids, with glycerine. An economical method of separating the acids and the glycerine was first discovered in 1831 by De Milley, who used lime for the purpose in place of potash and soda, the substances adopted by Chevreul and Gay-Lussac in their patents of 1825. The factory established by De Milley and Motard, near the Barriere de-l-Etoile, in Paris, gave the "Star Candles" their name. A candle is a simple but ingenious contrivance for supplying a flame with as much melted material as it can consume without smoking. If the thickness of the candle be properly adapted to that of the wick, the fatty matter immediately below the flame is melted, so that a cup-like reservoir is produced, always properly filled for feeding the flame. The fibers of the wick act as congeries of capillary tubes, which convey the fluid fat into the flame, where, being exposed to a high temperature, and sheltered from the air by the outer shell of flame, it becomes subjected to a dry distillation. The inflammable vapor thus produced rises, and by constant combustion, diminishes in quantity, and, consequently, in diameter, until at length it entirely

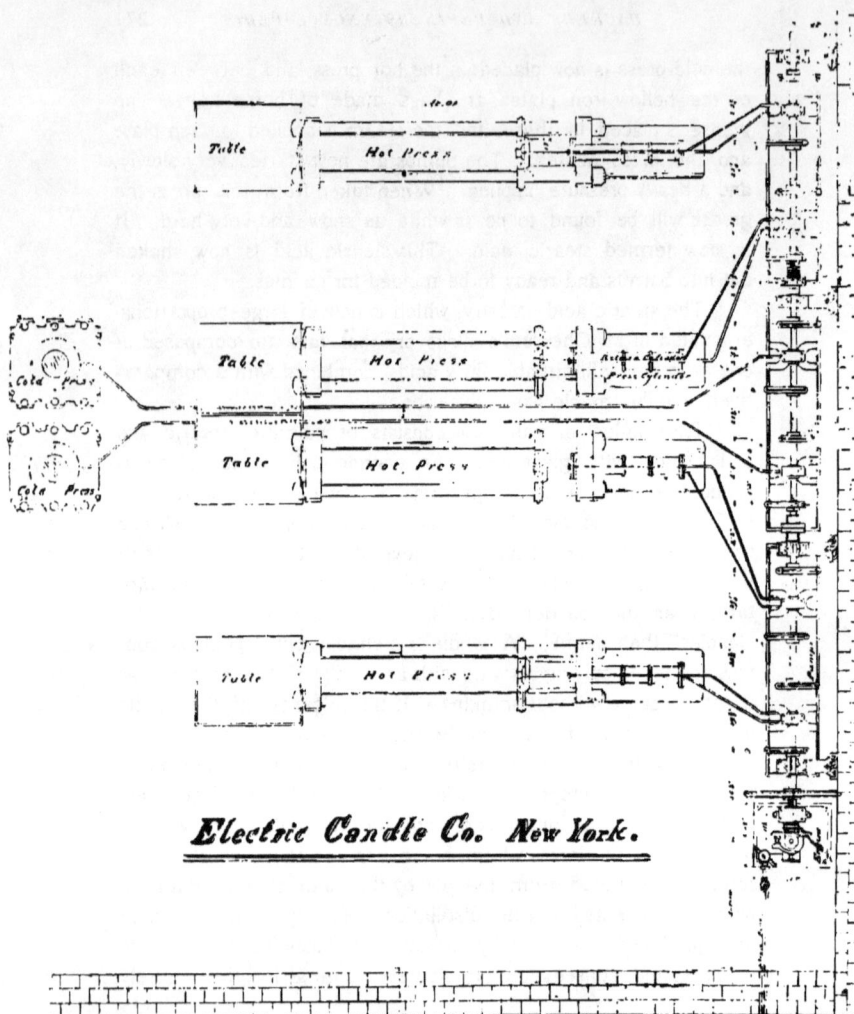

Table · Hot Press
Cold Press
Table · Hot Press
Cold Press
Table · Hot Press
Table · Hot Press

Electric Candle Co. New York.

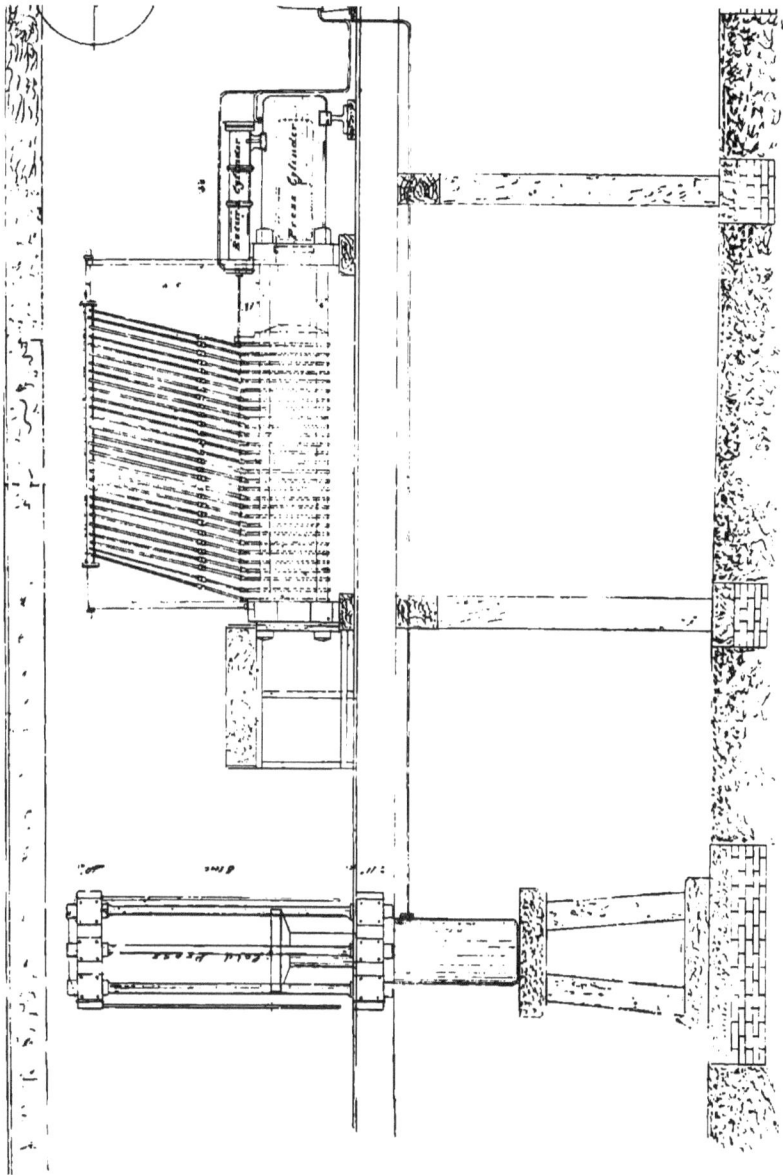

disappears in a point.   A current of air from below is produced
by the heat of the flame.   The oxygen of the air, aided by the
high temperature, decomposes the inflammable vapor of the fat
into hydrogen and carbon, and unites with these to form water
and carbonic acid.   The interwoven dark part of the candle, or
outer flame, contains unignited inflammable vapor, which will not,
of itself, support combustion, but may be drawn off with a glass
tube and ignited at a distance.

THE V. D. ANDERSON
DRYING MACHINES

The facilities of the butcher and packer are incomplete without appliances for utilizing the tankage and waste in such a way that they bring in their ratio of profit to the business, and in such conformity to proper sanitary conditions as to render their establishments unobjectionable to the community. The annoying features of the business still constitute a serious drawback to its successful and satisfactory prosecution, especially in towns where proper machinery for their effectual removal has not been introduced.

To the V. D. Anderson Company, of Cleveland, O., the packing house industry owe more for work done in its behalf than to any other concern in the same line of business in the country. Starting out a number of years ago with a DRYING MACHINE constructed on correct principles, they have added numerous improvements, suggested by a close study of the needs of the industry they have so successfully served, and by a long and varied experience, during which special needs and conditions have had to be provided for, and new adaptations made, until they are now able to supply the most perfect and effective machinery for the purpose to be found in the market, a statement fully borne out by the fact that all of the large packing house operators have adopted it in preference to other makes, and in many instances removing other machines to make room for it.

The important advantages possessed by the ANDERSON DRYERS are: 1. Thorough and economical manipulation of the material. 2. Complete drying power, whereby the strength of the fertilizer is preserved, waste or spoilage in handling prevented, and the safe delivery of the goods to the consumer assured. 3. Effective condensation of the steam generated by the drying process, thus doing away with all offensive odors. 4. Simplicity of construction, ease and economy of operation, with scarcely any liability to get out of order. The machines are made to meet the requirements of patrons, the size being determined by the amount of business done. The sizes and styles regularly manufactured are as follows:

The THREE CYLINDER DRYERS are made in two sizes, No. 1 and No. 2, and are set in brick work, to generate their own steam for drying.

The SINGLE CYLINDER MACHINES, embodying the same general principles as the three-cylinder, and adapted to the use of the smaller concerns, are made in four sizes,—No. 0, No. 1, No. 2, and No. 3. (See illustrations in advertisement.)

It is impossible within the limits of a single page to give a full description of our machinery, or even to do justice to those distinctive features which give it important advantages over that of other makes. We trust, however, that these statements will suffice to bring our machines to the notice of those not already familiar with them, and this being done, we are confident that their own needs and enterprise will prompt them to seek further information, and to add these needed facilities to their establishments. Information cheerfully furnished.

THE V. D. ANDERSON CO.,
Cleveland, O.

Makers of Fertilizer Dryers, Dryer Condensers, Tank Deodorizers, Pickers, Boilers, Tanks, Etc.

THE FRED W. WOLF
COMPANY

In this age of enlightenment and progressive ideas, nature seems in some instances to be almost outdone by artifice, and the Fred W. Wolf Co. appear to be determined to keep up with the band wagon in the procession. The firm of Fred W. Wolf was originally established on Lake Street, and was incorporated in 1887, with a capital stock of $250,000, Mr. Wolf having been chosen president. The following year they built their works at Hawthorne Avenue and Rees Street at a cost exceeding $250,-000 when fully equipped with machinery for turning out the famous Linde Ice and Refrigerating Machines, the United States patents for which are owned by Mr. Wolf. Their establishment is one of the most complete in the United States, having every appliance and labor-saving device to facilitate their work; but the business has increased to such an extent that it became necessary this year to make considerable additions to their already extensive works, and to expedite business they have moved their offices from 560 North Halsted Street to 121 and 123 Rees Street, where they have fitted up a spacious and well appointed suite of offices in a portion of the new addition to their factories. In addition to the ice-making and refrigerating machinery, they make an oil-extracting and gas-saving apparatus for ice-making and refrigerating machinery, valves for steep tanks, attachments

for refrigerating pipes, malt kiln floors and automatic malt-turning
machines; but the manufacture of the Linde Ice and Refrigerating Machine keeps them so busy that they have all they can do
to keep up with their orders.   This is not to be wondered at, as
the Linde is acknowledged to be the most efficient, simple, durable and economical for the production of refrigerating effects by
the compression and expansion of anhydrous ammonia.   It is
operated with less power, consumes less cooling water, and is
not affected by the ammonia used; is perfectly safe, the ammonia
being circulated in small quantities through iron pipes capable of
sustaining many times the pressure which they can possibly be
subjected to.   A novel application of artificial refrigeration will
be seen at the World's Fair, where the Fred W. Wolf Co. have
contracted with the Waukesha Hygeia Mineral Springs Co. to
cool drinking water that is piped over one hundred miles to the
Fair grounds, and deliver it cooled through forty or fifty miles of
pipe to the three hundred fountains on the grounds without loss of
its original pressure in the main pipes.   The cooling plant will
consist of two fifty-ton Linde machines, making a handsome and
complete exhibit.   The building is located east of the Sixty-fourth
Street entrance, opposite the "L" road terminus.   There are
over sixteen hundred Linde machines in actual operation, representing the capacity of over fifty thousand tons of melting ice
daily, and they are to be found in the largest and best equipped
packing houses and cold storage houses in this country, notably
those of Swift & Co., Cudahy Packing Co., Armour & Co.
G. H. Hammond Co., Western Refrigerating Co., etc., etc., etc

Index

W. A. CASE   W. G. CASE   G. A. WEGNER

THE CASE ❖ ❖

REFRIGERATING MACHINE CO.,

Ohio and Washington Sts., Buffalo, New York.

BUILDERS OF

Ice and Refrigerating Machines.

Our machines are the strongest built and most economical in the market, and are supplied with all improvements which a ten years' practical experience has suggested.

They produce a perfectly dry atmosphere and temperatures down to 20 degrees below zero if wanted.

We have furnished a large number of machines to packing houses and paraffine works.

Write for circular and obtain our prices before you order elsewhere.

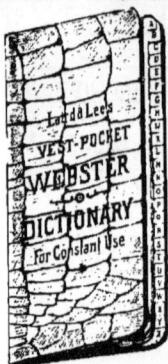

www.ingramcontent.com/pod-product-compliance
Lightning Source LLC
Chambersburg PA
CBHW020513270326
41926CB00008B/860